Quality Audits for ISO 9001:2000

Making Compliance Value-Added

Also available from Quality Press

ISO 9001:2000 Explained, Second Edition
Charles A. Cianfrani, Joseph J. Tsiakals, and John E. (Jack) West

Quality Audits for ISO 9001:2000: Making Compliance Value-Added
Tim O'Hanlon

ISO 9000:2000 Quick Reference
Jeanne Ketola and Kathy Roberts

ISO Lesson Guide 2000: Pocket Guide to Q9001:2000, Second Edition
Dennis Arter and J.P. Russell

ANSI/ISO/ASQ Q9000:2000 Series Quality Standards

ISO 9000:2000 for Small and Medium Businesses
Herb Monnich

The ISO 9001:2000 Auditor's Companion
Kent A. Keeney

The Practical Guide to People-Friendly Documentation
Adrienne Escoe

The Certified Quality Manager Handbook, Second Edition
Duke Okes and Russell T. Westcott, editors

Quality Audits for ISO 9001:2000

Making Compliance Value-Added

Tim O'Hanlon, Ph.D.

ASQ Quality Press
Milwaukee, Wisconsin

Library of Congress Cataloging-in-Publication Data

O'Hanlon, Tim, 1958-
  Quality audits for ISO 9001:2000 : making compliance value-added / Tim O'Hanlon.
    p. cm.
  ISBN 0-87389-530-4
  1. ISO 9000 Series Standards. I. Title.
  TS156.6 .O34 2002
  658.5'62—dc21

2001006576

10 9 8 7 6 5 4 3 2

ISBN 0-87389-530-4

Acquisitions Editor: Annemieke Koudstaal
Project Editor: Craig S. Powell
Production Administrator: Gretchen Trautman
Special Marketing Representative: Denise Cawley

ASQ Mission: The American Society for Quality advances individual, organizational and community excellence worldwide through learning, quality improvement and knowledge exchange.

Attention: Bookstores, Wholesalers, Schools and Corporations:
ASQ Quality Press books, videotapes, audiotapes, and software are available at quantity discounts with bulk purchases for business, educational, or instructional use. For information, please contact ASQ Quality Press at 800-248-1946, or write to ASQ Quality Press, P.O. Box 3005, Milwaukee, WI 53201-3005.

To place orders or to request a free copy of the ASQ Quality Press Publications Catalog, including ASQ membership information, call 800-248-1946. Visit our Web site at http://www.asq.org .

Printed in the United States of America

 Printed on acid-free paper

American Society for Quality

ASQ

Quality Press
600 N. Plankinton Avenue
Milwaukee, Wisconsin 53203
Call toll free 800-248-1946
Fax 414-272-1734
www.asq.org
http://qualitypress.asq.org
http://standardsgroup.asq.org
E-mail: authors@asq.org

To Sally,

Stephen,

Simon,

and Erin

for all those nights

when I was not at home.

Contents

List of Illustrations

Foreword

There is no doubt in my mind that the ISO 9001 quality system can be successfully applied to all kinds of companies, whether they are big or small. The correct implementation and evaluation of the system will significantly improve bottom-line results.

Based on my experiences at Grifo Enterprises, I am convinced that ISO 9001 certification is a powerful management process to improve one's business. My consultancy team and I have used ISO 9001 implementation to help a lot of companies become more effective and maintain recognition by their customers. Using ISO 9001:2000 to successfully improve results requires an understanding of quality processes and how to make the quality management system work to the advantage of the business.

A critical point in implementing a quality system based on ISO 9001 requirements is to be sure that quality audits are conducted in a meaningful and professional manner. A well-trained auditor is the main differentiator in determining whether an organization is investing or wasting money in evaluating the effectiveness of a system. Grifo Enterprises has arranged dozens of lead auditor courses with Dr. Tim O'Hanlon since 1992. His way of conducting a course is the "secret" of our success in this field. Tim O'Hanlon is the best consultant I know among very good professionals who implement and conduct lead auditor training courses.

We have found that the main concepts described by Tim in this book are the keys to successfully using audits as a tool to certify and improve an ISO 9001 quality system:

- A well-planned audit, irrespective of whether it is an internal, second-party, or third-party audit
- An experienced auditor to lead the audit team
- The audit team's abilities, competencies, and attitude while conducting the audit
- The understanding of the organization as a system
- The understanding of business processes

These concepts are easily understood; however, conducting a good audit is not as easy as it seems. I am convinced that using audits properly to certify or improve a quality system demands a well-trained and experienced auditor or team of auditors.

Tim knows, more than anyone, how to prepare an auditor to perform an excellent audit. All the Brazilians trained as auditors by Grifo Enterprises are delighted with Tim's ability to conduct their training and prepare them to do their jobs as auditors.

We at Grifo Enterprises are very grateful to have had the opportunity to know Dr. Tim O'Hanlon since 1992. We have become friends and will remain so forever.

I wish Tim a lot of success with this book. I am sure that he deserves it more than anyone.

Rosângela Catunda Cerqueira, Ph.D.
Vice President
Grifo Enterprises
Rio de Janeiro
Brazil

Preface

This book addresses the approaches used in quality management systems auditing, particularly third-party audits. It makes a valuable contribution to other types of audit processes as well, such as environmental systems auditing, and will be of benefit to internal and second-party auditors.

The purpose of the book is to attempt to refocus the traditional compliance-based audits toward a more value-adding process. Old school auditing was too concerned with issues such as calibration and document control, and while these are valuable attributes, the number of non-conformities raised against these requirements was disproportionate to their impact upon a business. Auditors owe it to their profession to use the new ISO 9001:2000 standard as an opportunity for a significant change in how they evaluate the implementation and effectiveness of quality management systems.

Following a review of the requirements of the standard we will work through each stage of the audit process, illustrating good practice and highlighting some of the things that can go wrong. The book will not, nor could it, provide all the answers, but it will make the reader think about how such situations might be handled. This time spent in proactive thinking may save some embarrassing moments in the future.

Particular emphasis has been given to developing meaningful checklists and value-adding reports—the latter becoming an ever-increasing requirement of discerning auditees. The use of case studies helps illustrate how value-adding reports can positively influence key performance indicators and how a structured approach to the development and deployment of policy and objectives can result in business improvement.

Some consideration is also given to those readers who are implementing a new or modified system and who act as internal auditors. Traditional-style auditors will not like this book, neither are they likely to understand it.

In the past 17 years, it has been my privilege to train several thousand potential auditors. My enthusiasm for the subject is as strong now as it was back in 1985. Performing value-adding audits is a satisfying role for any professional, and it is something in which I have a passionate belief.

Tim O'Hanlon
September 2001
Birmingham, England

Acknowledgments

This book is based on many years of auditing but particularly on the years spent around the world doing auditor training.

I would like to acknowledge my co-tutors in those courses:

Rosângela Catunda, Ph.D.	Márcia Martins
Edgard Cerqueira, Ph.D.	Alan Medley
Jorge Cerqueira, M.S.	David Osgerby
Carlos José Corrêia, Ph.D.	Noval D'Ávila
Mike Deare	Gilberto F. de Sampaio, M.S.
Maurice Jones	Brian Tilley, B.S.

There is, however, one tutor in particular upon whose course design work this book is largely based, and that is Alan Hurley. My special thanks to him for persisting with me.

My gratitude also to the following:

Molex Inc. and the staff of Molex Interconnect AG for use of the case study in Appendix A and to all other Molex employees involved in the implementation of TQM in Biberach, Shannon, and Ettlingen.

The ASQ members who reviewed the book and gave such encouragement and constructive feedback—Thomas A. Ratliff Jr., Steve R. Pollock, and Frank Sidorowicz.

Gilberto F. de Sampaio for his editorial comments.

The primary source of reference for this book is the QMS Auditor/Lead Auditor Course operated by Eurospan Developments Limited, U.K.

Where the term ISO 9001:2000 is used, it relates to ISO/ANSI/ASQ 9001:2000. Extracts from this standard have been used with the permission of ASQ and ANSI.

Where the term ISO 9000:2000 is used, it relates to the ISO/ANSI/ASQ 9000:2000 series. Extracts from this standard have been used with the permission of ASQ.

Introduction

Prior to reading this book, readers would do well to familiarize themselves with the following standards:

ANSI/ISO/ASQ Q9000-2000, *Quality management systems—Fundamentals and vocabulary*

ANSI/ISO/ASQ Q9001-2000, *Quality management systems—Requirements*

ANSI/ISO/ASQ Q9004-2000, *Quality management systems—Guidelines for performance improvements*

ANSI/ISO/ASQC Q10011-1994. *Guidelines for Auditing Quality Systems.* This standard will be replaced by BSR/ISO/ASQ QE19011, *Guidelines for quality and/or environmental management systems auditing* [currently available in draft format only].

No book or training course can make someone a good auditor, but it is hoped that the contents herein will prevent readers from being bad auditors.

CHAPTER **1**

Background

UNDERSTANDING QUALITY

Quality is an important issue for auditors to come to terms with. Too many auditors are well versed in the requirements of the ISO standard but have difficulty applying that learning in a practical business sense. The modern quality manager is more likely to be a skilled business person than the traditional chief inspector made good. Because of this it is important for auditors to speak on a captain-to-captain basis in terms universal to the field of quality—for example, statistical process control, the European Foundation for Quality Management (EFQM) excellence model, national quality awards such as the Malcolm Baldridge National Quality Award, and benchmarking.

Here is the new definition of quality found in ISO 9000:2000: *the degree to which a set of inherent characteristics fulfils requirements*. As with most definitions, it is not particularly helpful, but it gives us the basics—fulfilling requirements, whatever those might be and by whomsoever they were set. Auditors would do well to remember this most essential of points: systems are about ensuring the delivery of products or services that meet requirements.

QUALITY ASSURANCE IS A PREVENTIVE WAY OF THINKING

Quality assurance is not solely about control; it embraces all aspects of quality management—planning, control, and improvement. It is the part of quality management that brings structure. When we think of defining responsibility and authority, this is a proactive stance—as is training, selection of suppliers, process planning, document control, identification, traceability, and so on. Used as a preventive approach, quality assurance can add real value to a business. Used only as a control-based approach, it may prove a costly luxury.

1

THE ACCREDITATION AND CERTIFICATION PROCESSES

In Figure 1.1 we see the accreditation and certification processes. These are terms often misunderstood, even by auditors. Accreditation is the domain of the organizations that perform audits for the purpose of determining if companies are suitable for registration to the ISO 9001:2000 standard. Certification is the process by which all other organizations gain their certificate.

Figure 1.1 shows two processes: one for people that relates to how someone becomes a registered auditor or lead auditor through the International Register of Certificated Auditors (IRCA) or equivalent approved courses, and the second for organizations that want to become registered/certified to ISO 9001:2000. This second process is overseen in the United Kingdom by the United Kingdom Accreditation Service (UKAS) and in other countries by equivalent institutions ensuring that there are common interpretations and guidelines applied internationally.

Figure 1.2 shows the process of certification used by the accredited organizations. Some of the steps vary between one accredited body and another, but this basic process is the one that we will be referring to throughout this book.

The two major activities of the audit cycle are the adequacy audit, which determines whether the documented system meets the requirements of the reference criteria—normally ISO 9001:2000—and the compliance audit, where the audit team verifies the implementation and effectiveness of the documented system.

In this book we explore each of the steps in this cycle; and, indeed, the cycle forms the majority of the chapter headings.

Preassessment visits are not always practical, but they are helpful to both the auditor and auditee. This will be discussed further in chapter 5.

The compliance audit consists of four major steps:

1. The opening meeting
2. The execution of the audit
3. The closing meeting
4. The report

These are covered in chapters 8 through 12; follow-up and surveillance visits are covered in chapter 13. Thus Figure 1.2 will serve as our road map through the audit process and through this book.

The final chapter of the book addresses the future of auditing and the necessary changes required in the field of auditing if the audit process is to gain credibility in the eyes of upper management.

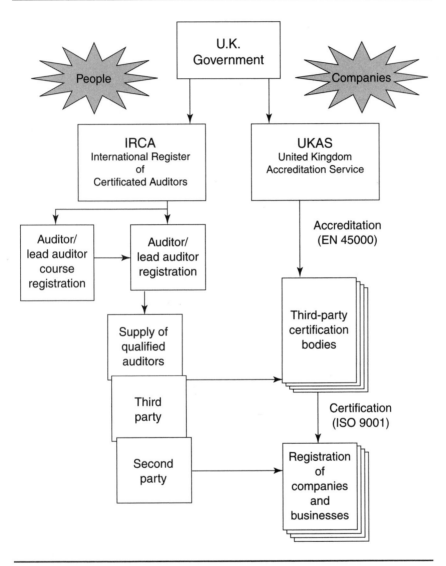

Figure 1.1   Accreditation and certification processes—U.K. model.

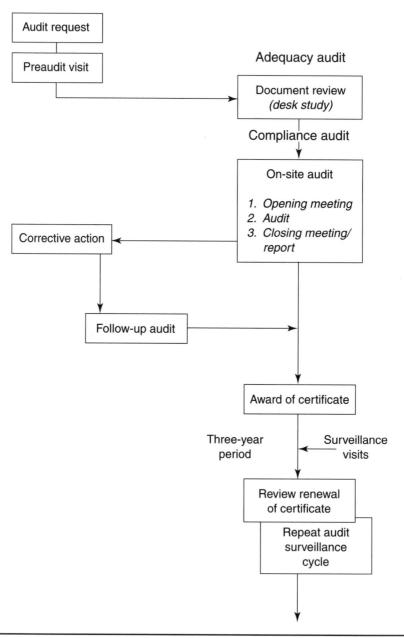

Figure 1.2 The audit cycle (basic cycle—certification of quality systems).

The book concludes with a case study of an organization in the Netherlands that used the audit process as a mechanism to drive continuous improvement. Other appendices include the lessons learned by over one thousand potential auditors who have completed the Eurospan Developments Limited Lead Auditor course.

In another case study we will see one approach to developing policy and objectives and how they may be deployed. This is to facilitate auditing this aspect of a business, which may be a new challenge for auditors.

Of course, not all organizations will be registered to ISO 9001:2000, and a typical action plan for implementing ISO 9001:2000 is included for reference.

Finally, a job description for an internal auditor has been prepared to show the responsibilities and knowledge required for this fundamental element of any quality management system.

CHAPTER 2

Understanding the Requirements
of ISO 9001:2000

BACKGROUND ON THE STANDARD

The new version of ISO 9001, released in December 2000, is now the only standard against which third-party quality system audits may be performed for the purpose of ISO certification. (Note, however, that there is a period of overlap between the 1994 version of the standard and that of 2000 until 2003.) The latest revision is the most radical in terms of restyling the standard.

Certainly much of the background of ISO 9001:2000 lies in the electronics and military arenas. The defense standards of the 1960s and 1970s such as O5-21 and the Allied Quality Assurance Publications (AQAPs) were amongst the forerunners in the evolution of the standard. When the British Standards Institute (BSI) unveiled its BS 5750 in the late 1970s, it was a significant milestone in the life of quality professionals. Further revisions in 1987 and 1994 saw the ISO 9000 series of standards gain international acceptance, and during the remainder of the 1990s the bad press about the bureaucracy of the standard and its lack of impact on the bottom line led to the scheduled latest revision in December 2000. This was also consistent with routine reviews of such standards every five years.

The current versions of the ISO 9000 series of standards are as follows:

- ISO 9000, *Quality management systems—Fundamentals and vocabulary*
- ISO 9001, *Quality management systems—Requirements*
- ISO 9004, *Quality management systems—Guidelines for performance improvements*

PURPOSE OF THE STANDARD

Although ISO 9001:2000 is not a product specification, it does serve to create a set of working practices that if applied correctly will lead to products and services meeting defined requirements.

The standard may be used as a reference for competent auditors to determine if specific clauses in the standard are implemented and effective.

This may be done by third parties for the purpose of registration; by second parties to determine the suitability of potential vendors or existing suppliers; or in-house to determine the ongoing suitability and effectiveness of a company's own quality system. Although the standard is partially prescriptive in its use of the term *shall*, it is possible to exclude clauses (although only from clause 7 of the standard) or adapt them to the particular environment. To this end the standard is equally suitable to service and manufacturing organizations.

THE LOGIC OF QUALITY MANAGEMENT SYSTEMS

The year 2000 version of the standard removed a major criticism of earlier versions by reducing the emphasis on the need for documented procedures. The new standard requires just six:

- Document control
- Records
- Control of nonconforming product
- Audit
- Corrective action
- Preventive action

These documented procedures are in support of other process documentation deemed necessary by the organization.

A quality management system should be evaluated for effectiveness, and this is usually done once or twice a year as part of the management review process. For this evaluation to be meaningful the system should have measurable objectives that have been aligned and integrated with overall policy and strategy. Failure to integrate the system with overall business objectives often leaves the system as a "bolt-on" package.

The foundation of quality management systems is that objectives are defined; approaches for achieving those objectives are documented; the satisfaction of stakeholders with the outcomes is measured; and actions are taken to improve continually. This is a logic that is difficult to counter.

UNDERSTANDING THE REQUIREMENTS

It is always dangerous to offer one's own interpretation of a standard; there are always those with different interpretations, even amongst the audit fraternity. This is not a bad thing, but it is inevitable. The remainder of this chapter consists of two parts: first, some tree diagrams to show how ISO 9001:2000 is structured and, second, a commentary on some of the changes in the new version based on the questions frequently asked in auditor training courses. This provides a backdrop against which the focus of this book—the audit process—can be seen.

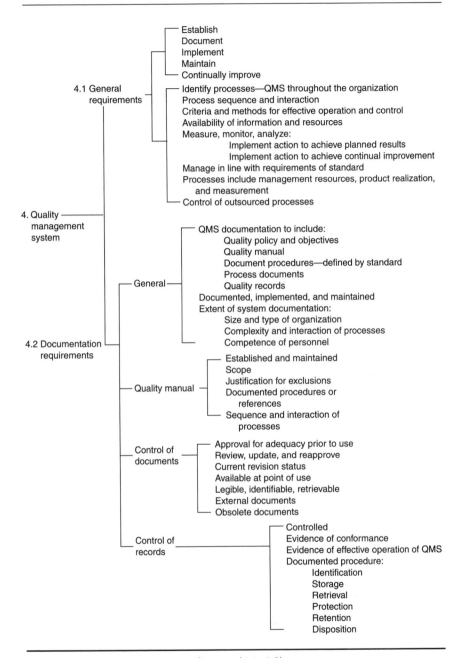

Figure 2.1   ISO 9001:2000 tree diagram (4.1–4.2).

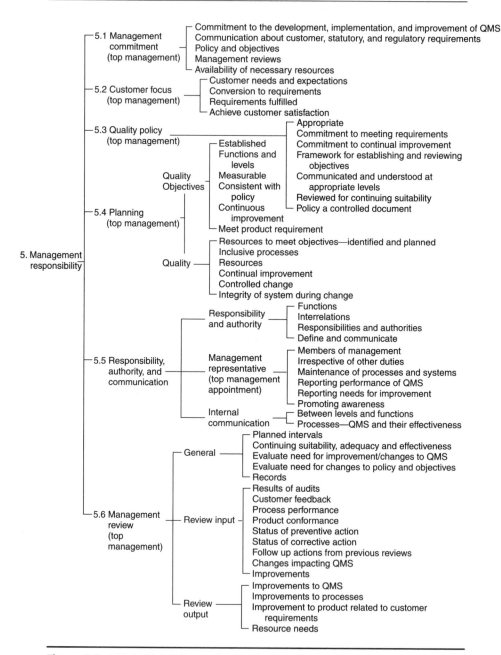

Figure 2.2   ISO 9001:2000 tree diagram (5.1–5.6).

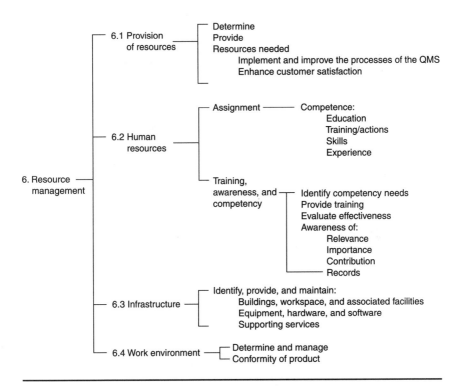

Figure 2.3   ISO 9001:2000 tree diagram (6.1–6.4).

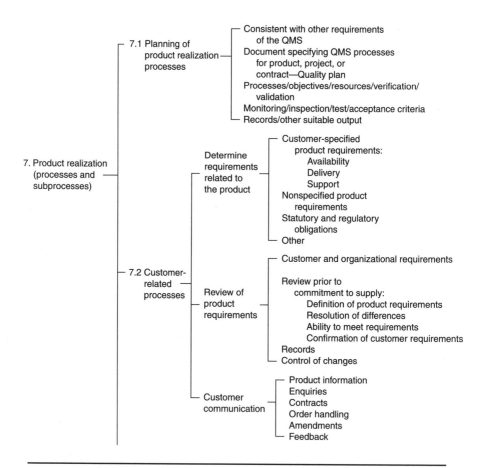

Figure 2.4 ISO 9001:2000 tree diagram (7.1–7.2).

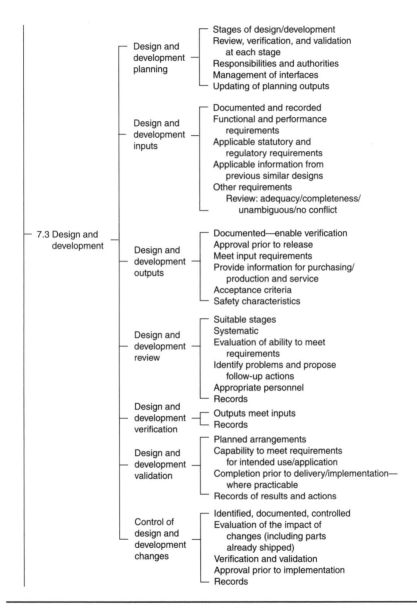

Figure 2.5   ISO 9001:2000 tree diagram (7.3).

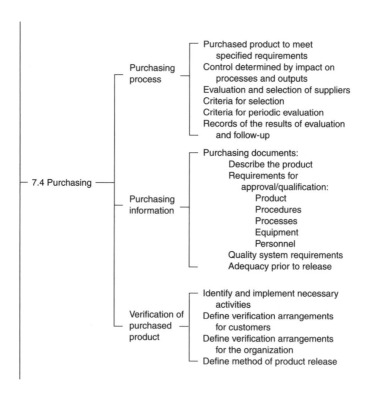

Figure 2.6 ISO 9001:2000 tree diagram (7.4).

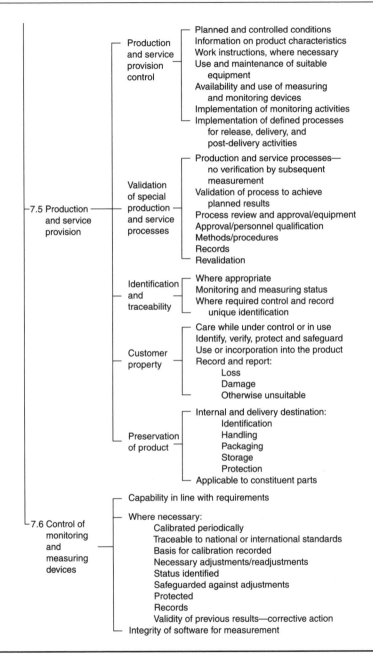

Figure 2.7   ISO 9001:2000 tree diagram (7.5–7.6).

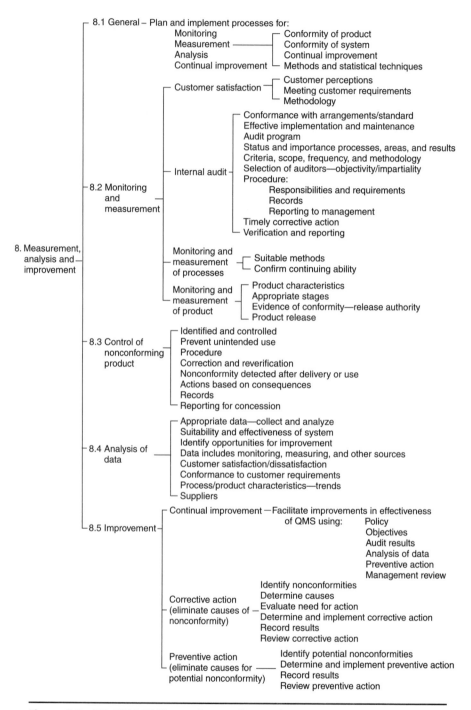

Figure 2.8   ISO 9001:2000 tree diagram (8.1–8.5).

FREQUENTLY ASKED QUESTIONS

Q1. Does ISO 9001 certify products?

A. No. ISO 9001 certifies systems, but the purpose is to ensure that products and services meet specified requirements.

Q2. What is meant by "a process-based approach"?

A. Organizations must recognize that the achievement of product conformity is the consequence of a series of interrelated activities. These activities combine to form processes; the bringing together of processes is described as the system. Each process has defined inputs, outputs, resources, and controls. Management of the processes and their interactions is what is termed the process-based approach.

Q3. What is meant by "scope"?

A. Scope relates to those activities within the boundaries of the system and includes the applicable standards, documents, contracts, products, processes, personnel, and locations. Further guidance is given in the document ISO/TC176/SC2N/524R2 (found on the World Wide Web at www.iso.ch).

Q4. What is meant by "outsourced processes"?

A. Outsourced processes may include those activities essential to the completion of a product or components thereof that are undertaken by suppliers or subcontractors.

Q5. What is the difference between documents and records?

A. Documents describe what must be done and are usually prepared before an event. Examples are contracts, standards, quality manuals, procedures, work instructions, and specifications. Records are the proof of what has been done and are thus produced after an event (for example, training records, audit reports).

Q6. What is the difference between "policy" and "objectives"?

A. Policy is a general statement of intent (for example, "to achieve customer satisfaction"), whereas objectives are expressed in measurable terms (for example, "to achieve 99.9 percent on-time delivery performance").

Note: Auditors need to have an appreciation of how policy and objectives are formulated in businesses and how they are subsequently deployed within the business. See Appendix C.

Q7. Does the ISO 9001:2000 mandate the need for work instructions?

A. No. The standard mandates the existence of a quality manual, procedures for document control, records, control of nonconforming product, internal audit, corrective action, and preventive action plus the necessary process documentation. Work instructions may be used at the discretion of the auditee, where they are considered necessary.

Q8. Does the standard specify what records have to be maintained?

A. Yes. See Table 2.1.

Q9. How does an organization decide whether procedures or process documents are required?

A. This is determined by the type of company, the complexity of the processes, and the competence of the personnel.

Q10. Do we have to put an organizational chart in the quality manual?

A. No, although responsibilities and authorities must be defined somewhere in the system. Although not mandatory, it is helpful to include an organizational chart and matrix of responsibilities. The mandatory contents of a quality manual are as follows:

- The scope of the system
- Justification for any exclusions
- The documented procedures or reference to them
- A description of the interaction between the processes of the quality management system

Table 2.1 Records required by ISO 9001:2000.

Clause	Record required
5.6.1	Management reviews
6.2.2(e)	Education, training, skills, and experience
7.1(d)	Evidence that the realization processes and resulting product fulfill requirements
7.2.2	Results of the review of requirements relating to the product and actions arising from the review
7.3.2	Design and development inputs
7.3.4	Results of design and development reviews and any necessary actions
7.3.5	Results of design and development verification and any necessary actions
7.3.6	Results of design and development validation and any necessary actions
7.3.7	Results of the review of design and development changes and any necessary actions
7.4.1	Results of supplier evaluations and actions arising from the evaluations
7.5.2(d)	As required by the organization to demonstrate the validation of processes where the resulting output cannot be verified by subsequent monitoring or measurement
7.5.3	The unique identification of the product, where traceability is a requirement
7.5.4	Customer property that is lost, damaged, or otherwise found to be unsuitable for use
7.6	Results of calibration and verification of measuring equipment
7.6(a)	Standards used for calibration or verification of measuring equipment where no international or national measurement standards exist
7.6	Validity of previous results when measuring equipment is found not to conform with its requirements
8.2.2	Internal audit results
8.2.4	Evidence of product conformity with the acceptance criteria and indication of the authority responsible for the release of the product
8.3	Nature of the product nonconformities and any subsequent actions taken, including concessions obtained
8.5.2	Results of corrective action
8.5.3	Results of preventive action

Source: International Organization for Standardization, ISO/TC176/SC2/N525R, Annex B, www.iso.ch.

Q11. What is meant by the term "document control"?

A. Document control is defined in clause 4.2.3 as follows:

(a) to approve documents for adequacy prior to issue;
(b) to review and update as necessary and reapprove documents;
(c) to ensure that changes and the current revision status of documents are identified;
(d) to ensure that relevant versions of applicable documents are available at points of use;
(e) to ensure that documents remain legible and readily identifiable;
(f) to ensure that documents of external origin are identified and their distribution controlled; and
(g) to prevent the unintended use of obsolete documents, and to apply suitable identification to them if they are retained for any purpose.

Q12. How long must records be kept?

A. This is determined by legislation, customer requirements, and/or the organization itself.

Q13. What is top management responsible for?

A. Top management's responsibilities are defined as follows:

- Demonstrating commitment—that is, communicating to the organization the importance of meeting customer as well as statutory and regulatory requirements, establishing the quality policy, and ensuring that quality objectives are established (clause 5.1)
- Customer focus (clause 5.2)
- Quality policy (clause 5.3)
- Objectives (clause 5.4.1)
- Quality management system planning (clause 5.4.2):

  (a) the planning of the quality management system is carried out in order to meet the requirements given in clause 4.1, as well as the quality objectives, and
  (b) the integrity of the quality management system is maintained when changes to the quality management system are planned and implemented.

- Responsibility and authority (clause 5.5.1)
- Management representative (clause 5.5.2)
- Internal communication (clause 5.5.3)
- Management review (clause 5.6.1)

Q14. How do we audit the appropriateness of the quality policy?

A. Examine how the organization has integrated the quality policy with overall policy and strategy (for example, look for objective evidence that quality policy is aligned with other aspects of policy such as reducing cycle time on new product introduction).

Q15. What is meant by "providing a framework for establishing and reviewing quality objectives" (ISO 9001:2000 clause 5.3[c])?

A. The management review process has to determine the effectiveness of the quality management system. To do this, the quality policy needs to be converted from statements of intent to measurable objectives.

Q16. As an auditor, how do I determine if the quality policy is understood within the organization (ISO 9001:2000 clause 5.3[d])?

A. Interview individuals at various levels in the organization to determine if they can explain how they contribute to the achievement of the overall policy (ISO 9001:2000 clause 6.2.2[d]).

Q17. What is meant by establishing quality objectives at relevant functions and levels (ISO 9001:2000 clause 5.4.1)?

A. Most quality objectives are determined at a strategic level. For example, you might determine that you want to achieve a delivery performance of 99.9 percent on time. But what does that mean to the sales department? Perhaps for the sales team it would be the number of orders that are accepted in accordance with the agreed-upon lead time. In the quality department this may translate to the number of production shipments inspected on the same day as they are produced.

Q18. Does an organization have to have job descriptions?

A. No. Responsibilities and authorities can be defined in a number of ways (for example, matrices, procedures, flowcharts, or job descriptions).

Q19. Does an organization have to have a quality manager?

A. There is no mandate to have someone with the title "quality manager." ISO 9001: 2000 is very clear in clause 5.5.2(a).

Q20. Does the auditor have to evaluate the effectiveness of the organization's communications processes?

A. Regarding the effectiveness of the system, yes. Typically, the auditor is looking for an examination of how the organization establishes the communications needs of the business from internal and external sources. The communications process should then proceed to demonstrate how the organization filters the various types of information and decides, "Who needs what?" It is then necessary to show how the information is deployed to the right people in a timely manner. The measurement processes should take into account the timeliness of the communications process and the effectiveness of the process (that is, do the recipients understand the information and what they are to do with it)?

Q21. How often does the organization have to perform a management review?

A. There is no specified frequency, but auditors should challenge the rationale of the frequency that has been specified by the organization.

Q22. What should a management review cover?

A. See ISO 9001:2000 clauses 5.6.2 and 5.6.3.

Q23. How can an auditor evaluate the appropriateness of the resources defined by the organization?

A. This is not a valid audit question. The auditor should ask the auditee how it determines that the resource levels are appropriate, and then determine if that level of resources has been provided.

Q24. Do training records have to be established for everyone?

A. No, but records should show that people are qualified based on education, training, skills, and experience.

Q25. Does the effectiveness of training have to be evaluated?

A. Yes. See ISO 9001:2000 6.2.2(c).

Q26. Does ISO 9001:2000 address health and safety requirements?

A. Not directly. But "the organization shall determine and manage the work environment needed to achieve conformity to product requirements" (ISO 9001:2000 6.4).

Q27. What is the difference between clause 5.4.2, "Quality management system planning," and clause 7.1, "Planning of product realization"?

A. In clause 5.4.2 the focus is the overall system. In 7.1 the focus is clearly the planning of the product definition, design, manufacture, delivery, and service.

Q28. Are the quality objectives cited in clause 7.1(a) the same as those required in clause 5.4.1?

A. There is some overlap, hence the cross-reference in clause 5.4.1. However, in 5.4.1 the focus is all the quality objectives. In clause 7.1(a) the focus is solely the product-related objectives.

Q29. What is meant by "acceptance criteria" in clause 7.1(c)?

A. Acceptance criteria can be dimensions on a drawing, master samples of color, or codes of conduct in a service company. It is the definition in unambiguous terms of what is acceptable.

Q30. What is the difference between clause 7.1, "Determination of product requirements," and clause 7.2, "Review of product requirements"?

A. In clause 7.2.1 an organization must gather all the sources of data that define what the product is (for example, customer, legislative inputs). In clause 7.2.2 the organization is assessing whether it can meet these requirements.

Q31. Where differences in contract requirements from those previously expressed are resolved, does this have to be in writing?

A. There has to be a record of the resolution of differences.

Q32. If an organization knowingly accepts a contract that it knows it cannot meet (for example, delivery dates), is this a nonconformity?

A. Yes. Part of the review of requirements is to ensure that the organization has the ability to meet requirements (ISO 9001:2000 7.2.2[c]).

Q33. How can a telesales organization whose customers buy from a catalog keep records of every telephone call it receives?

A. Many organizations face the same challenge. Calls are often received where potential customers are just making inquiries, and those never turn into orders. The organization must establish some criteria to determine when the formal review begins. In the case of the telesales organization, it would be when the customer says, "I want to order product X." The telesales person can then work through an on-screen checklist, filling in boxes as each question is answered. This on-screen record becomes the evidence of the review.

Q34. Very often a customer specifies that he or she wants something and promises to confirm it in writing but never does. How should this be addressed?

A. Typically this can be done as an order acknowledgment or an acknowledgment to an amendment. Many organizations do this for all transactions so that they have some objective evidence that the transaction took place.

Q35. How should an organization deal with a customer who keeps changing an order?

A. A process must be in place for controlling such changes, thus avoiding the customers getting the wrong product or multiple variations of the product. Auditors will examine the communications processes in such circumstances and the integrity with which the older orders are canceled.

Q36. How should an auditor determine the effectiveness of the customer communications processes?

A. The first issue is to understand how the auditee determines the effectiveness of the process. Therefore, the auditor should look for some evidence of a plan-do-check-act (PDCA) cycle. Regarding planning, how were the customer communications needs determined? What was the planned process to deliver those needs? How does the organization measure the effectiveness of the process (for example, percentage hit rates on advertising or sales visits, percentage of orders processed without an error, level of customer complaints per million transactions, customer satisfaction with the complaint cycle time, effective resolution of the problem)?

Q37. In design and development (clause 7.3) should an organization include the design of its service or other business processes?

A. That is not the intent of the standard, but if "product" includes "service" then the design and development of service processes definitely needs to be considered. This is why the scope of the audit is so important. Clause 7.2.3(b) of the standard specifically states that "design and development outputs shall provide appropriate information for purchasing, production and for service provision." The design outputs are the translation of the design inputs into some measurable or tangible criteria. It is difficult to understand how a service organization can thus exclude its service processes from this clause. In fact, any organization providing a service element in its business must justify excluding this clause from its system.

Q38. The requirements in clause 7.3.1 sound as though they are just good project management approaches. Is this a correct interpretation?

A. Yes. All project plans need to specify what has to be done, by whom, by when, using what resources, and which organizational structure; the review and control requirements; and the communications processes. This needs to be kept up-to-date as the design evolves.

Q39. I do not understand what "inputs" in clause 7.3.2 means.

A. Design inputs are sources of information used by the designers to create the design. Inputs can include technical reports, historical information about previous designs, customer tenders, market reports, research and development data, and/or legal or statutory requirements. One of the initial design reviews will examine these various inputs to create a clear and precise product definition.

Q40. Design outputs are what exactly?

A. What design outputs are "exactly" is difficult to say because they will vary from one organization to another, but typically they include drawings, specifications, standards, and methods.

Q41. What are "reference criteria"?

A. Reference criteria can be dimensions on a drawing or a color swatch, or the set of behaviors for a service provider. They need to be measurable (for example, if something has to be "clear," how "clear" is "clear"?).

Q42. When clause 7.3.3(d) says to "specify the characteristics of the product that are essential for its safe and proper use," I assume this means the finished product.

A. Not necessarily. Some components may have sharp edges or "Class A" surfaces that must be protected. Packaging materials may contain plastic bags, which would be dangerous to children. Containers may be too heavy to lift without special equipment. In this situation it is better to be safe than sorry. Compensation in a product liability lawsuit or an industrial injury claim could be a very expensive consequence of not getting this part of the design output right.

Q43. How often should design reviews be performed?

A. As often as necessary and more specifically as often as they were scheduled to happen in the design plan (ISO 9001:2000 7.3.1).

Q44. Does a design review have to be conducted by people who are independent of the actual design work?

A. No, but it realistically should include such people. As design review is a multifunctional activity many people are involved. This is the issue for the auditor: Who gets involved, at what stage, and what is the rationale for this decision?

Q45. Please explain the difference between design verification (clause 7.3.5) and design validation (clause 7.3.6).

A. Design verification is a theoretical proving of the integrity of the design. For example, a senior designer will take the drawings for all the mating components and after evaluating them will decide that they will "in theory" work. This is one method of verification. In other words, do the design outputs address the design inputs? Other methods include design simulations or comparisons with previous designs. This does not, however, ensure that the end product will do what the end user wants it to do. This second assessment is the "practical" examination of the product through the eyes of the end user and may include, for example, the evaluation of prototypes or the commissioning of a new computer system by the user with a period of debugging before the product is paid for.

Q46. What happens if the verification activities or the validation activities prove the product does not work?

A. The auditor, in these circumstances, must look for two things:

- What corrective action was taken on the product design and is there evidence that this action was subsequently accepted?
- What corrective action was taken on the design process, particularly the verification stage, to determine why this failure was not detected and to ensure that this "escape route" is closed for subsequent designs?

Q47. Are design verification and validation stages mandatory?

A. They are part of clause 7 (where requirements can be excluded), but if the other stages of the design requirement are applicable, the auditee has to justify why verification or validation is not. That would be an interesting discussion!

Q48. Are separate controls necessary to control design changes compared with changes in other documents (for example, the quality manual)?

A. The personnel involved will probably be different, but the controls will be similar (for example, as defined in ISO 9001:2000 4.2.3).

Q49. Clause 7.3.7 states the following: "The review of design and development changes shall include evaluation of the effect of the changes on constituent parts and product already delivered." What does that mean?

A. If a product is changed (for example, perhaps a safety fault was detected), those involved in the design changes need to think about products that are already in service. Should they be recalled and modified? Perhaps there are components in stock or raw materials that need to be modified or scrapped. This review should be documented, and the decision formally recorded. Auditors will clearly seek to build a link in such circumstances with the corrective action process (ISO 9001:2000 8.5.2) and the controls for identification and traceability (ISO 9001:2000 7.5.3).

Q50. Is the purchasing process (clause 7.4.1) applicable to all purchased products and services?

A. Not necessarily. The organization has to decide for each product or service or family thereof what controls it determines are necessary.

Q51. Does an organization have to have an "Approved Suppliers List"?

A. There is no mandate to have a document in the system with that title. There is a requirement to have "records of the results of evaluations and any necessary actions arising from the evaluation" (ISO 9001:2000 7.4.1). How an organization chooses to achieve this outcome is up to it. From an auditor's point of view, one is seeking a clear indication of how a buyer knows who to buy from and on what basis that supplier has been selected. If there is a list defining the supplier, the product, and approval criteria, that makes everybody's life easier.

Q52. Can you list some of the criteria that an organization might use to select suppliers?

A. There are many options:

- Proven history of performance
- Registration to ISO 9001:2000
- Subject to the findings of goods inwards inspection
- Subject to certificates of conformity
- Supplier quality assurance audit by the organization
- Customer mandate
- Self-assessment report by the supplier

Q53. What is meant by reevaluation of suppliers?

A. Reevaluation of suppliers may be accomplished by repeating a supplier quality assurance audit every year or six months. It may be done through an automated vendor appraisal process, which is updated each time the quality details of a delivery are entered. It may be done through an annual self-assessment. There are too many possibilities to list. What is being sought is evidence that the selection criteria are still applicable. The frequency of the reevaluation will be determined by the criticality of the supplier, the frequency of supplies, and the history of performance. Whatever is done regarding reevaluation, the results thereof and the subsequent actions must be recorded.

Q54. In clause 7.4.2(a), (b), and (c), very specific contents of the purchasing information are defined. Is this mandatory?

A. No. All of these attributes are included where appropriate.

Q55. Does purchasing information (for example, purchase orders) have to be signed before release?

A. There needs to be evidence of review and approval before the purchasing information is sent to the supplier. This does not necessarily mean a signature.

Q56. I don't understand the purpose of clause 7.4.3.

A. The verification of purchased product means that the auditee's organization or its customers need to make the necessary arrangements for verifying products being provided by (or the systems of) the supplier. In some cases the customer (the end of the supply chain) performs audits of the suppliers (the start of the supply chain). If the customer does "approve" the supplier, that does not mean that the organization can abdicate its responsibility for controlling the supplier.

Q57. Which business processes are under the scope of clause 7.5.1?

A. Those processes specifically associated with the production of or the servicing of the product defined in the scope of the system.

Q58. In clause 7.5.2 there is a reference to the validation of processes. Can you give some examples of such types of processes?

A. In previous versions of the standard, such processes were known as "special processes." Examples might include welding, enameling, or heat treatment. For such processes, the auditor will look for evidence that the inputs to the process and the process conditions are controlled rather than the output of the process.

Q59. Is it true that identification and traceability are not mandatory?

A. As far as ISO 9001:2000 is concerned, identification is required "where appropriate," and traceability is necessary where it is a requirement. Identification defines what a product is and is often done through labels or bar codes. Traceability is often achieved through batch numbers. The customer, the law, the industry, or the organization itself may define traceability requirements. Traceability may be used to limit product recall in the event of a problem.

Q60. What examples can you give me of "customer property"?

A. In a hospital, customer property might be the patient's valuables handed over to the hospital to store while the patient is there. In a hotel, customer property might be clothes submitted for laundry. In a manufacturing company, examples could include raw materials or packaging supplied by the customer as "free issue" material.

Q61. If a customer supplies raw material that is used by the organization and it subsequently proves to have been faulty, who is responsible—the customer or the organization?

A. Subject to what is specified in the contract, the organization is responsible and therefore should contract some sort of incoming controls on products supplied by the customer.

Q62. Does the preservation of product extend to raw materials, components, and subassemblies?

A. Yes. When considering the scope of "preservation," auditors need to consider the contractual obligations of the organization, the pertinent legislative requirements in addition to the requirements of the standard, and the organization's system. It is important to understand, contractually, where the organization's responsibility for preservation begins and ends.

Q63. Where does the organization's responsibility for preservation of product end?

A. Wherever the contract documentation says it ends.

Q64. Does all process and measuring equipment have to be calibrated?

A. Although it is sensible to calibrate any device used for measurement purposes, ISO 9001:2000 specifies in clause 7.6 that such controls are undertaken on "monitoring and measuring devices needed to provide evidence of conformity of product to determined requirements (see 7.2.1)."

Q65. Please explain clause 7.6(a).

A. Clause 7.6(a) contains two requirements. First, equipment must "be calibrated or verified at specified intervals, or prior to use." There is no mandate for what the frequencies should be, but that will be influenced by the criticality of the equipment, its sensitivity to variation (known through research or analysis of records), and the frequency with which it is used.

Second, this calibration must be "against measurement standards traceable to international or national measurement standards; where no such standards exist, the basis used for calibration or verification shall be recorded." This means that the integrity of the calibration must be evident. Traceability in this context relates to the trail of records that can be followed showing the chain of equipment used in the calibration process right back to the reference source (for example, the standard meter of light in the National Physical Laboratory). Such traceability is normally indicated by quoting the serial numbers on the certificates of calibration of each piece of equipment in the chain. However, for some equipment no such standards exist. It is thus for the organization and its customers to agree upon a form of calibration that is mutually acceptable and consistent. This process must be recorded. The auditor must also be satisfied that this process demonstrates integrity of the results.

Q66. What is meant in clause 7.6(c) by enabling the calibration status to be determined?

A. Simply that anyone using a piece of equipment should know, perhaps through labeling, that the equipment has a valid calibration status (for example, when it was last calibrated, when it is due for its next calibration).

Q67. What should an organization do if a piece of equipment fails calibration?

A. The organization should have a defined process for identifying the extent of the error and then making decisions about the severity of the error and the subsequent action. Any action taken should be recorded.

Q68. Can an auditor insist that a company use statistical techniques?

A. No, but the auditor can ask for a justification of why such techniques are not used.

Q69. What type of monitoring, measurement, and improvement processes should an auditor be seeking?

A. There are three primary types: those that indicate conformity of the product, those that indicate conformity of the system, and those that indicate the continual improvement of the system. See ISO 9001:2000 8.1(a-c).

Q70. To meet the requirements of clause 8.2.1 must the organization do a customer survey?

A. The term "customer survey" can mean many things (for example, written questionnaires, interviews with critical customers, focus groups). So to insist on this term is not appropriate. However, the organization must have some mechanism for capturing and addressing customer perceptions.

Q71. How often should an organization obtain information on customer perceptions?

A. At a frequency that it has determined to be appropriate based on historical evidence, frequency of transactions, and the results of previous evaluations. It may be appropriate to gather perceptions for the lifetime of the product to determine perceptions with reliability.

Q72. How often should the system be audited by the organization's own auditors?

A. At a frequency that is commensurate with the scope of the system, historical performance of previous audits (for example, areas or processes that receive more nonconformities than others should be audited more frequently), and the importance of the activity. These frequencies are usually set during the management review meeting but may be changed if the scope is changed or if there are some known problems (for example, an increase in customer complaints).

Q73. What should the focus or objectives of an internal audit be?

A. To determine the effectiveness of the system, to examine the extent of conformity with planned arrangements, to verify the level of implementation, and to identify opportunities for improvement. See ISO 9001:2000 8.2.2(a and b).

Q74. Can someone audit his or her own work?

A. Not if he or she wishes to comply with the requirements of ISO 9001:2000. People should be encouraged to examine their own work, but this is not acceptable as a means of meeting the internal audit requirement of the standard.

Q75. What is meant by the term "undue delay" when describing the time scale according to which management must respond to the findings of the internal audit?

A. The organization should include some criteria for determining appropriate time scales for responding to nonconformities. This may be based on the severity of the problem (for example, those issues leading to a negative impact on product conformity should be addressed immediately and may require work in progress to be reverified).

Q76. The 1994 version of the standard devoted a large section (clause 4.10) to inspection and testing. This is not evident in the new standard. Why is this?

A. It is true that the level of detail in respect to this topic is substantially reduced, but the principle still remains as seen in ISO 9001:2000 clauses 8.2.3 and 8.2.4. The emphasis now is on the organization's determining, during the planning stage (clause 7.1), what controls are required for ensuring that processes and products meet planned arrangements. The auditor can challenge the rationale for such decisions in order to be satisfied that such controls are adequate.

Q77. If a company has a final inspection process, is it true that one of the checks to be performed is to ensure that all the previous inspections and tests that are in the plan have been performed?

A. ISO 9001:2000 clause 8.2.4 specifies, "Product release and service delivery shall not proceed until the planned arrangements (see 7.1) have been satisfactorily completed, unless otherwise approved by a relevant authority and, where applicable, by the customer." Your suggestion seems a sensible way of ensuring this.

Q78. Where in the process do the controls for nonconforming product apply?

A. Nonconforming product can be generated anywhere in the process (for example, in purchased goods or materials), in the organization, or in transit or as a result of a customer complaint or rejection. The controls are equally applicable in any of those stages. The auditor should refer to the contract and the scope of the system.

Q79. Does nonconforming product that has been repaired have to be reinspected?

A. It has to be reverified, which may constitute some form of inspection.

Q80. Clause 8.4(a-d) specifies those data that have to be analyzed. Are these the only types of data for the purposes of ISO 9001:2000 that have to be collected and analyzed?

A. No. Earlier in the section the standard states, "The organization shall determine, collect and analyze appropriate data to demonstrate the suitability and effectiveness of the quality management system and to evaluate where continual improvement of the effectiveness of the quality management system can be made." The term *appropriate* means that the organization, in addition to the types of data specified in 8.4(a-d), must determine other data needed in its system.

Q81. What is the difference between corrective action and preventive action?

A. Corrective action is taken after an event, when something has gone wrong. It focuses on eliminating the cause of the problem so that it cannot happen again. Preventive action happens before an event and focuses on eliminating the possibility of a problem ever happening. It is thus proactive rather than reactive.

Q82. What are the links between the eight quality management principles and ISO 9001:2000?

A. The eight quality managment principles are discussed in the next section. Here is the correlation between each principle and ISO 9001:2000.

Principle: Customer focus

Clause: 5.1(a), 5.2, 5.3(b), 5.5.2(c), 5.6.2(b), 5.6.3(b), 6.1(b), 6.3, 7.2.1(a), 7.2.1(b), 7.5.4, 7.5.5, 8.2.1, and 8.4(a)

Principle: Leadership
Clause: 5.1, 5.2, 5.3, 5.4.1, 5.4.2, 5.5.1, 5.5.2, 5.5.3, 5.6, and 6.2.2

Principle: People
Clause: 4.1(d), 5.1(a), 5.1(e), 5.3(d), 5.4.1, 5.5.1, 5.5.2, 5.5.3, 5.6.3(c), 6.1, 6.2, 6.4, 7.2.2, 7.2.3, 7.3.1, 7.3.4, 7.4.2, 7.5.2(b), 8.2.2, and 8.3

Principle: Processes
Clause:

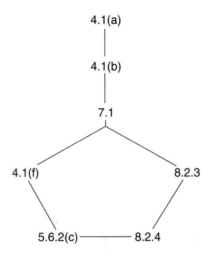

Principle: Continuous improvement
Clause: 4.1, 5.1, 5.3(b), 5.4.1, 5.6.1, 5.6.2(g), 5.6.3(a), 5.6.3(b), 8.1(c), 8.2.2, 8.4, 8.5.1, 8.5.2, and 8.5.3

Principle: Data
Clause: 5.4.1, 5.4.2, 5.6.1, 8.1, 8.2.1, 8.2.3, 8.2.4, 8.4, 8.5.1, 8.5.2, and 8.5.3

Principle: Systems
It can be argued that all requirements are applicable, but specific reference is made to the system in the following clauses: 4.1, 4.2.1, 4.2.2, 4.2.3, 4.2.4, 5.1, 5.3, 5.4.2, 5.5.2, 5.5.3, 5.6.1, 5.6.2, 5.6.3, 6.1, 7.1, 8.1, 8.2.1, 8.2.2, 8.2.3, 8.4, and 8.5.1

Principle: Suppliers
Clause: 7.4 and 8.4

Q83. One of the new requirements of the standard is "internal communications" (ISO 9001:2000 5.5.3). We are struggling in our organization to define a process for this.

A. Most organizations in the world have a problem with communications—they have many methods of communication but often lack an integrated, overall approach. Typical steps include these:

- Establish the communications needs internally and externally (clauses 5.5.3 and 7.2.3)
- Establish the internal and external data available (clause 8.4)
- Collect and prioritize the data and identify those stakeholders who require this information
- Benchmark the communications process
- Design processes for cascading the information
- Develop measures to determine the timeliness and effectiveness of the communications process
- Continually refine the communications process

THE EIGHT QUALITY MANAGEMENT PRINCIPLES (SEE ISO 9000:2000)

Auditors would do well to keep in mind the eight quality management principles when using the ISO 9001 standard as the audit reference criteria. Herewith are the eight principles and a short explanation of each:

1. *Customer focus.* Understand and meet customer needs and expectations.
2. *Leadership.* Provide unity and direction and the internal environment necessary to achieve business goals.
3. *Involvement of people.* Use the skills and expertise of the organization's people to meet business goals.
4. *Process approach.* Manage resources and activities as a process. Figure 2.1 is a representation of the process approach depicted in ISO 9001:2000, and it illustrates how the various elements of the standard are used to convert business inputs to business outputs (products and services) and how feedback from customers is used to drive continuous improvement. It is a logical deployment of the plan-do-check-act cycle.
5. *System approach to management.* Coordinate the process activities to enable the organization to operate both effectively and efficiently.

6. *Continual improvement.* Make continual improvement one of the permanent objectives of the organization. Auditors should seek objective evidence of this.

7. *Factual approach to decision making.* Ensure that the organization uses data generated from measurement and learning activities to make decisions.

8. *Mutually beneficial supplier relationships.* Use partnership arrangements to enhance the value-adding contribution of the relationship for both buyer and seller.

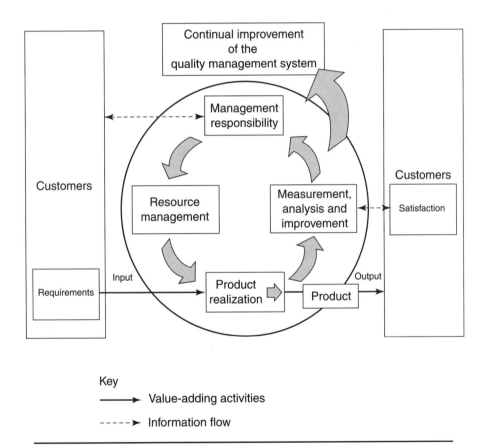

Figure 2.9 The process approach (ISO/ANSI/ASQ Q9001-2000).

CHAPTER 3

Quality System Documentation

DOCUMENTING A QUALITY MANAGEMENT SYSTEM

There may be 50 ways to leave your lover, but there are many more ways of documenting a quality system. This section describes several typical approaches auditors may come across.

Organizations should not seek merely to document the system as it is now but should strive to create the system as it should be, and that should be evident through a structured approach to review and continual improvement.

Methods available for documenting the system vary from the traditional pile of manuals to the more modern electronic or intranet-based systems. The latter cause some problems for auditors because gauging the complexity of the system becomes more difficult. In one case, an auditor discovered that within a year the auditee's intranet system had evolved into some 1.2 million pages. This shows a basic lack of understanding on the part of the auditee of document control. Hard copy or electronic, there can be no free license to produce documents at will. The adequacy audit covered in chapter 5 explains how to ensure that the auditee's documented system meets the requirements of ISO 9001:2000.

The structure of the quality system is important to understand for it enables the auditor to be selective in those aspects considered critical to the system's successful implementation and effective operation.

Figure 3.1 shows that the procedures and process documents exist to ensure policy and objectives are met. The records are the proof that this transformation has happened and that stakeholder requirements have been satisfied. The *typical* documentation hierarchy is shown in Figure 3.2.

ISO 9001:2000's lack of emphasis on documented procedures does not mean that the process methodologies do not need to be defined in some way. Otherwise what is there to audit? Or is everything that has been pontificated by the audit fraternity over the past 30 years now to be dismissed?

The quality manual will define policy and objectives; the mandatory procedures will provide evidence of control in key areas; and the process

4.2.1 Documentation requirements

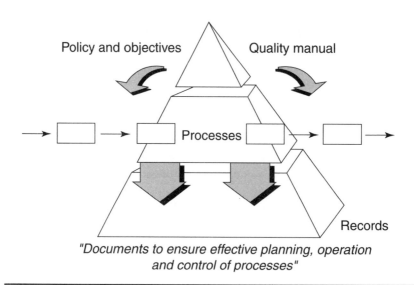

Policy and objectives

Quality manual

Processes

Records

"Documents to ensure effective planning, operation and control of processes"

Figure 3.1 Documenting a system.

Source: Eurospan Developments Ltd. QMS Auditor/Lead Auditor Course 2000, section 6. Used with permission.

4.2.1 Typical Quality System Document Hierarchy

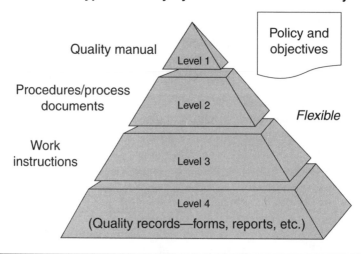

Quality manual

Policy and objectives

Level 1

Procedures/process documents

Level 2

Flexible

Work instructions

Level 3

Level 4

(Quality records—forms, reports, etc.)

Figure 3.2 Typical documentation hierarchy.

Source: Eurospan Developments Ltd. QMS Auditor/Lead Auditor Course 2000, section 6. Used with permission.

documents will show how the organization operates and links these operations with overall policy and objectives. Records are the objective evidence that what is claimed actually happens.

It is through the internal audit and management review processes that an organization can determine whether the defined procedures and methodologies are being followed and whether they are achieving the stated objectives. This is the stimulus for continual improvement.

Three key words determine the extent of the documentation in the quality system:

- Company—the nature of the business, the type of sector, the reasonable expectations of a company of this type
- Complexity—the type of products, services, and processes involved, the level of automation
- Competency—the knowledge, skills, attitudes, and behaviors of the workforce

THE QUALITY MANUAL

Figure 3.3 shows the mandatory requirements in relation to the quality manual. The quality manual serves little purpose in the organization on a day-to-day basis, but it does provide the direction and overall structure of the system. It enables the auditor to begin to develop a first level of understanding regarding the nature of the auditee's business. The scope is particularly useful as it places in context the boundaries within which the audit is to be performed.

4.2.2 The Quality Manual

- Established and maintained

- Scope

- Exclusions

- Procedures or references

- Sequence and interaction of processes

- Controlled document

Figure 3.3 The quality manual.

Source: Eurospan Developments Ltd. QMS Auditor/Lead Auditor Course 2000, section 6. Used with permission.

THE DOCUMENTED PROCEDURES

There are now six mandatory documented procedures according to ISO 9001:2000:

- Document control (clause 4.2.3)
- Control of quality records (clause 4.2.4)
- Internal audit (clause 8.2.2)
- Control of nonconformity (clause 8.3)
- Corrective action (clause 8.5.2)
- Preventive action (clause 8.5.3)

Such procedures not only need to be documented but should be implemented and maintained. They are living documents and should show evidence of continual improvement.

DOCUMENT CONTROL

No documented system is complete without the procedure for controlling the various documents in the system (for example, the quality manual, procedures, process documents, work instructions, standards, and specifications). The basic controls include the following:

- Approve prior to use.
- Review, update, and reapprove.
- Identify the current revision status.
- Make available at point of use.
- Ensure documents are legible, identifiable, and retrievable.
- Include pertinent external documents.
- Prevent unintended use of obsolete documents.

Note that auditors need to be conscious of the various approaches used to manage obsolete documents (for example, shredding, incineration, archiving in a file that clearly indicates that the documents are obsolete). The key is to remember the purpose of managing obsolete documents—that is, to prevent their inadvertent use.

CONTROL OF RECORDS

Again, there are basic controls for all the records in the system, and these are used to provide objective evidence of product conformity and system compliance.

- Implement a procedure for controlling the records
- Identify the records to be kept
- Store in suitable facilities
- Ensure legibility, including over time
- Ensure records are retrievable within a suitable time frame
- Protect against damage or deterioration
- Retain as required by law, the customer, or the organization itself
- Dispose at the end of the period of retention, respecting confidentiality as appropriate

Note: When considering the examination of records, auditors must be aware of what they are looking for. For example, when examining an engineering change note, is there evidence of consideration of customer satisfaction, cost implications, impact on resources, impact on work in progress, impact on products already in use, and impact on the system? When examining a corrective action request, is there evidence that the effectiveness of the corrective action has been established? When looking at calibration records, is there evidence of traceability to national or international standards (where these are necessary), and is there evidence that unsatisfactory results have resulted in corresponding corrective action?

CHAPTER 4

Background on Auditing

UNDERSTANDING THE AUDIT PROCESS

An early understanding of the term *audit* can be found in the following description: "An audit is an official examination of accounts by references to witnesses and vouchers." This description is useful because it emphasizes three issues:

- The need for the audit process to be official and thus have credibility with upper management
- The need to speak with people
- The importance of examining objective evidence

ISO 9000:2000 defines *audit* as a "systematic, independent and documented process for obtaining audit evidence and evaluating it objectively to determine the extent to which audit criteria are fulfilled."

Again, systematic refers to the need for the audit process to be structured and purposeful. Independence ensures that there is no bias in the process, and the evaluation of findings needs to be objective and based on objective evidence. In this way the auditor can determine if the objectives of the audit have been met.

THE THREE TYPES OF AUDIT

Although the majority of this book focuses on the approaches of third-party auditors—those performing audits to determine the suitability of an organization to become registered to ISO 9001—the reader should understand the three types of audit:

- *Internal, or first party.* Members of an organization examine their own organization.
- *Second party.* A customer audits a supplier at some point in the supply chain (that is, it could be your customer auditing you or you auditing your supplier).
- *Third party.* This audit is usually done for the purpose of certification by representatives of independent organizations.

The auditee's need in all of these processes is the same: the auditor adds value. As much emphasis needs to be placed on the adequacy and effectiveness of the system as on adherence to procedures or process documents.

TRADITIONAL CRITERIA-BASED AUDITING

It has not been uncommon for auditors to use the 20 requirements of ISO 9001:1994 as their checklist. The standard says, "Thou shalt," and the auditor says, "Show me that you do." This is a criteria-based audit—turning the requirement of the standard into a question. An example of such a checklist is included in chapter 6.

This type of audit, though comprehensive, often missed the point of what auditing is about. Too much emphasis was placed on adherence to the words of the standard and not enough on the value-adding contribution or effectiveness of such compliance.

Strictly following the requirements of the standard often simulates "auditing in boxes," as depicted in Figure 4.1. Each function represented by a box can be accomplishing the things specified in the procedures, but the end result, the outcome of the process, is wrong. This is because many processes are designed function-by-function and not as an overall, end-to-end process. Criteria-based auditing can miss the problems caused by transactions at interface points. The new process approach can be truly successful only if we move away from criteria-based auditing and toward process-based auditing. This is discussed further in chapter 6. It suffices for now to note that auditors must understand the basic premise of the simple process model as shown in Figure 4.2.

The weakness of criteria-based auditing

Adherence to procedures versus conformity of output

Figure 4.1   Criteria-based auditing.

Source: Eurospan Developments Ltd. QMS Auditor/Lead Auditor Course 2000, section 7. Used with permission.

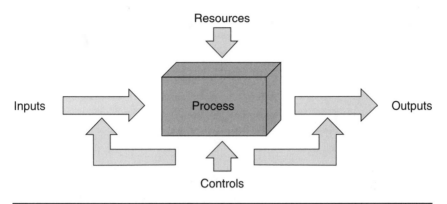

Figure 4.2   The simple process model.
Source: Eurospan Developments Ltd. QMS Auditor/Lead Auditor Course 2000, section 7.
Used with permission.

As this model shows, the auditor must grasp five attributes along the entire process:

- What are the inputs from one process step to the next?
- What are the activities in this step of the process?
- What resources are used, and how are they planned and monitored?
- What controls are used to ensure that process activities are sustained in accordance with requirements?
- How is the output measured for conformity?

INTEGRATED SYSTEMS AUDITING

As organizations continue to restructure and resources become ever more tight, it will be necessary to broaden the scope of audits (for example, use the same personnel to perform quality, safety, and environmental audits). This in turn will facilitate organizations in the integration of their systems.

MOVING AWAY FROM A FOCUS ON PAPER

Clearly the majority of auditors and auditees understand the need to reconsider the emphasis on creating a mountain of paperwork. Auditing is much more than just looking at documents and records.

Auditors need to satisfy themselves that the organization's people have clear responsibilities and levels of authority in reality, not just on paper. Management must have confidence that process and legislative requirements are being satisfied as well as the needs and expectations of other stakeholders.

AUDITING STANDARDS

General

It is a certain trend that although the level of documents (for example, procedures, work instructions) in an organization will reduce, the level of records is unlikely to change very much. Records may be more scientific now and even be in an electronic format, but they will persist in the same numbers. This is of interest to the auditor of course, but what is of greater value is understanding how the organization uses the data contained in those records to drive continual improvement.

The application of the auditing standards (ISO 10011 to become ISO 19011) which are complimentary to the ISO 9000 series has been of some value to the consistency of the audit process, particularly the parts that have focused on the actual methodologies of the audit process.

Reasons for Initiating an Audit

Having experienced the audit process from both sides, many auditors and auditees question why they put themselves through such torture. There are reasons for this masochism:

- Audits are valuable to determine whether a potential vendor has the capacity to meet an organization's needs.
- Audits may be used to determine whether a company is meeting its own system requirements or a customer's; not all audits have ISO 9001:2000 as their reference criteria.
- Audits may be used to ensure continuing compliance and effectiveness of a system during the lifetime of a system or contract. Everyone knows that organizations can look good for a day, but can they sustain it for the long term?
- Finally, one can initiate an audit to determine if an organization meets the requirements of ISO 9001:2000 and may thus be considered for certification.

Understanding the Audit Scope

Woe betide the auditor who does not clearly understand the scope of the audit. The term *scope* is used to encapsulate the products, processes, standards, documents, contracts, locations, departments, and personnel who fall under the umbrella of the audit.

The scope of an organization's certification is recorded on its certificate or an attachment thereto. The scope is particularly important in the context of "exclusions"—that is, the capacity for an organization to exclude some of the requirements from its system.

Understanding the Audit Objectives

There is typically a range of five audit objectives:

- Improvement
- Conformity
- Effectiveness
- Regulation
- Registration

Where improvement is one of the objectives, it changes the nature of the audit process. This is common to internal or first-party audits. This is not to say that in certain second-party audits a customer representative might not provide some advice, but that will depend on whether the potential vendor may be used or not. In third-party auditing giving advice is taboo, so although improvement is a natural consequence of responding to nonconformities, we should take care that we do not confuse our true objective as third-party auditors.

The goal of conformity is common to all audit types—first, second, and third party. Conformity means ensuring adherence to procedures, standards, contracts, and other pertinent documents.

Effectiveness, too, is common to all audit types. In measuring effectiveness, the auditor determines if the system is enabling the organization to achieve its objectives and the needs and expectations of the stakeholders.

Regulation typically falls in the domain of third-party organizations such as legislative institutions (for example, safety or environmental) and not usually in that of organizations involved with ISO 9001 certification. Internal audits may of course address such requirements, as might some customer audits.

And finally, registration applies, in this understanding, to those organizations that are performing audits to determine whether an organization can be recommended for inclusion on a register of organizations that meet the requirements of ISO 9001.

Understanding the Audit Plan

Understanding the audit's scope and objectives is an important aspect of compiling the audit plan. As an audit is a process involving interaction between auditors and auditees, the audit team needs to know who the key players are in the organization. Lists of names and job titles are not always that helpful as job titles often give no indication of the responsibilities of the individual concerned.

Although the audit is not just about documents, the auditor does need to understand the documents required to perform the audit. These might include the following:

- Standards
- Quality manual
- Procedures, process documents, and work instructions
- Master lists
- Brochures and catalogs
- Contracts
- Specifications

A sometimes frustrating part of the planning process is bringing together a suitable team. This means coordinating a mixture of skills, personalities, and available and independent people. Some team members may not be specialists in ISO 9001 or indeed in the audit process, but they may be technical specialists on the team where complex processes are involved. Every audit combines a mixture of two languages: the technical language of the business and the language of the tongue. Using a specialist may overcome the former, and an interpreter the latter.

The basic requirements of the audit plan are the administrative issues, as follows:

- Date
- Time
- Duration
- Number of auditors
- Location
- Shift patterns
- Security and parking arrangements

Mastering these details will enable the audit team to begin the process of putting together a detailed program of interviews for the execution of the audit. We will revisit this in chapter 6.

The requirement to clarify the restrictions in the area of confidentiality has become common. It is good practice to never discuss the audit findings of one organization with any third party, but some organizations may require the audit team to sign confidentiality or nondisclosure agreements. It is always worthwhile to have a legal specialist review these, just in case.

The audit report must also be considered during the planning phase. What style is required? Who will receive copies? When is it required?

Understanding the Lead Auditor's Responsibilities

Simply put, the lead auditor is responsible for everything associated with the audit process. That includes the planning and preparation, the opening meeting, coordinating and participating in the audit, the closing meeting, deciding on nonconformity classifications, preparing the report, and ensuring that there is a follow-up to close out the audit.

During planning and preparation the lead auditor must clarify the audit's scope and objectives, ensure that checklists are prepared, pull together the program of interviews, and gather the necessary information and documentation from the auditee. This planning stage is particularly important if the audit is taking place in a region or country different than the auditor's own. The lead auditor must become acquainted with the local culture—perhaps by contacting the appropriate embassy or a local agent.

Where possible, it is a good idea for the lead auditor to be involved in the selection of other team members. This is more likely to result in a cohesive team.

As mentioned, the audit plan and program of interviews need to be defined and agreed upon with the other members of the audit team and the auditee's representative. Such communication should be confirmed the day before the audit, ensuring that there are no last-minute hitches.

Checklists are an important part of the audit process, and although the lead auditor does not prepare all the checklists personally, his or her role is to ensure that they are comprehensive and make the best use of the team's resources. In this way, clear responsibilities are assigned to each auditor with a defined scope of activities to be covered.

The one skill the lead auditor must have in his or her tool kit is the confidence to deal with senior managers as well as with people at all levels of the organization. This is particularly true when a dispute arises during the audit process.

The chairing of opening and closing meetings is covered in more detail in chapters 8 and 11 respectively.

The lead auditor's role concludes with the raising and classifying of nonconformities, issuing the audit report, and arranging follow-up audits. These are all covered in the later chapters 10 and 13.

Understanding the Auditor's Responsibilities

Naturally the lead auditor assumes the role of an auditor in most audits in addition to the responsibilities of leadership. He or she is an additional member of the team.

The auditors, where required and logistically practical, will participate in each phase of the audit—planning, opening and closing meetings, conducting the audit, preparing nonconformity reports, and follow-up. Sometimes the audit commences on different sites at the same time, so parallel opening meetings may be required. Occasionally the audit concludes on different sites, and it is impossible for the entire audit team to get back to one location for the closing meeting. The team's findings must be telephoned through if necessary.

Where several auditors are involved in an original audit and nonconformities are raised, it is not necessary for all the auditors to go back for the follow-up visit.

The auditors must comply with the audit requirements assigned by the team leader. These may be specific requirements, processes, or rules of the game.

Communication skills are an essential part of the auditor's profile, and these are important within the audit team as well as with the auditee. Although the lead auditor will make most of the contacts during the initial preparation stages, auditors must clarify their additional needs with the auditee. It can be embarrassing for the auditee if an auditor with special needs turns up without any prior notification.

The key word for any auditor is *professionalism,* and this quality embraces the execution of tasks effectively and efficiently.

A common weakness of auditors is their failure to record findings in sufficient detail to be able to manage challenges later. Documenting the numbers of products, names of people, locations, and reference numbers of documents is a discipline that auditors must master.

Once findings have been made and agreed upon with the auditee's representative, the auditor may be required to present findings at the closing meeting. This makes sense, as it is the auditor who was present at the time of the finding. If the lead auditor presents all the findings, questions will have to be deferred to the relevant auditor anyway.

As mentioned earlier, the entire audit team is unlikely to return for the follow-up visit, but one or more team members may be required to revisit the auditee organization to verify the implementation and effectiveness of any corrective action.

A golden rule for auditors is understanding and respecting the need for and expectation of confidentiality. This extends not only to the findings of the audit but also to privileged information disclosed during the audit and to any documentation provided.

One thing auditors, particularly third-party auditors, should not do is give advice. Their primary role is to perform an audit against established criteria and obtain objective evidence.

Understanding the Responsibilities
of the Auditee's Management Team

By this stage in the evolution of the use of audits it is unlikely that a management team will not know what to expect from an audit, but this is something to be confirmed rather than assumed.

Perhaps during the initial contact, during the preaudit visit, or in the confirming correspondence the lead auditor will ensure that there are no misunderstandings about who does what (for example, that the management team needs to ensure that all employees know the scope and objectives of the audit and the part that each of them may be expected to play). Managers must not intimidate employees with threats about the consequences of negative audit findings.

A clear demonstration of how seriously the management team takes the audit is the people that it appoints as guides. If those people are unsuitable they can compromise the smoothness of the audit.

The management team must also think through the audit process and how it can ensure that it presents the organization in the most realistic light (for example, ensuring that there are parking spaces for the audit team, that the names of the auditors are on the welcome board, and that meetings are started on time and people are made available when required).

If the organization's managers see the process as one of partnership they will ensure that an environment of cooperation prevails. This might include the provision of an office, telephones, fax machines, canteen, computer, intranet site, documents, and the necessary facilities required to perform the audit.

Finally, the auditee's management team must understand that it is the ones responsible for identifying and implementing the corrective action in response to any nonconformities. In other words, the auditors are not consultants!

Finalizing the Audit Team Selection

As mentioned, the audit team must have a combination of the right audit skills, ISO 9000 knowledge, and understanding of the auditee's products and processes. All the team members must be independent, and the auditee has the right to decline the involvement of any particular auditor, with a justifiable reason.

One factor to consider with regard to the availability of the auditors at the time of the audit is their current workloads.

In addition, the team leader must be a good communicator, organizer, and coordinator capable of being a firm but fair arbitrator when the need arises.

Aborting an Audit

This most unpleasant of circumstances—aborting an audit—is rare, but the protocols involved must be understood. An audit may be aborted because the achievement of the audit objectives are compromised, the organization being audited does not have a quality system (one might have been documented but not implemented), or there are too many nonconformities. There is no magic number for the latter outcome, and it is influenced by how far the audit has progressed in the audit schedule (for example, five nonconformities on the last day of the audit would not justify aborting the audit, but 20 in the first morning probably would). In the third-party situation the auditee will end up paying for the auditor's time whether it is used or not so the auditee is justified in asking for the audit to be completed.

The protocol for aborting an audit calls for contacting the person or body commissioning the audit and advising them of the circumstances. If they agree an abort situation exists, the lead auditor will call a premature closing meeting and advise the auditee of the circumstances and the next steps.

CHAPTER 5

Initial Preparation

THE PERTINENT DOCUMENTATION

The matrix in Table 5.1 clarifies what documents are required for each type of audit. Those documents highlighted in bold are the primary documents in each audit type.

These documents cannot serve as the basis of the audit in isolation. They must be put in the context of the business's objectives, the process inputs and outputs, and the nature of the business.

SCOPE AND EXCLUSIONS

Since the advent of ISO 9001:2000, the clarity with which the scope and exclusions are determined has become even more important. Let us remind ourselves what is meant by these two terms.

The term *scope* is used to encapsulate the products, processes, standards, documents, contracts, locations, departments, and personnel who fall under the umbrella of the audit. This enables the audit team to devote its resources to those activities within the scope of the audit. The

Table 5.1 Audit documentation matrix.

	Contract	*Standard*	*Manual*	*Procedures/ process documents*	*Instructions*	*Other*
First-party audit	Yes	Yes	Yes	**Yes**	Yes	Yes
Second-party audit	**Yes**	Possibly	Yes	Yes	Sometimes	Yes
Third-party audit	Yes	**Yes**	Yes	Yes	Yes	Yes

linkage with the *exclusions* factor is important because organizations need to clarify why they have excluded certain requirements in the standard's product realization clause from the scope.

Audit teams must never begin the audit process until the scope and exclusions are understood and agreed upon.

INITIAL CONTACT AND GATHERING INFORMATION

Breaking the ice with the potential auditee is always a nervous moment, as the auditor is never quite sure what type of welcome he or she will receive. Fortunately, the majority of organizations act professionally and are polite if not totally welcoming. It is important to make human contact as soon as is practical, and not rely solely on e-mail, fax, or letter. The best mode of contact is undoubtedly the preaudit visit, where this is logistically feasible, as it allows participants to meet face-to-face and begin building that so important rapport.

The good auditor obtains as much meaningful information about the auditee organization as is practical. This can include:

- visiting the business's Web site;
- reviewing newsletters;
- reviewing annual reports;
- reviewing product catalogs; or
- viewing corporate videos.

Once the auditor has gained a picture of the organization, additional documentation such as the following can be obtained and reviewed:

- Quality manual
- Procedures
- Process documents
- Organizational chart
- Lists of names of key people
- Location map
- Site drawing showing size and layout of key areas

In return, it is good practice to formally document the audit process for the auditee, explaining the protocols involved and the audit team's expectations (for example, attendees at the opening and closing meeting; access to fax, phone, office).

THE PREAUDIT VISIT

Many auditors agree that the advent of the year 2000 version of the standard has probably increased the amount of time required to plan and conduct an audit, particularly if the auditee wants the process to be value adding. The need for the auditor to analyze and understand the process documents has also increased the significance and value of the preaudit visit.

The opening day of an audit can be difficult if auditors have no prior understanding of the auditee company or its products or processes. This sense of awe can be greatly reduced if the audit team can make an earlier, less formal visit. The preaudit visit is mutually beneficial to both auditor and auditee. For the auditor it greatly enhances the planning process, and it is typically the lead auditor who conducts the visit. For the auditee, its managers can begin to grasp the type of individuals that they are dealing with.

The preaudit visit is also mutually beneficial because it verifies that an auditable situation exists. Whilst it is not a consultancy process, it does enable the partnering process to begin and the establishment of ground rules. If there is clearly no established system it may be futile to proceed with the formal audit. It is the "sense" of the organization that the auditor finds most valuable, the "feel" for what type of organization is being presented.

Making human contact must not be underestimated in terms of its value to ensuring a smooth audit process (for example, knowledge about personal protective equipment, safety rules, security requirements).

Without the cloud of the formal audit hanging over the two parties, the lead auditor and, typically, the management representative can resolve issues that can cause problems on the day of the audit (for example, they can clarify scope and exclusions, confirm the status of documents, and agree on a process for notifying the audit team of any changes made to documents before the day of the audit).

Each auditee presents a new set of culture, politics, and expectations, and the preaudit visit enables these to be appreciated.

Finally, the ability to physically survey the process without the preoccupation of the checklists is of great benefit to the final planning stages of the audit, especially if there are specialist or complex processes.

THE ADEQUACY AUDIT

Sometimes called the "desk study," the adequacy audit usually follows the preaudit visit and is conducted in the office of the audit team. The purpose of the adequacy audit is to determine whether the documented system adequately addresses the requirements of the standard. It enables the nominated audit team member to consider the scope and exclusions and discuss them with the team—gaining further clarification from the auditee if necessary. It is usual for only one member of the team to conduct the desk study, reviewing his or her findings with the other team members. It is also necessary for each team member to read the quality manual as a means of orientation prior to preparing check lists and conducting the compliance audit.

The evaluation of the quality manual and procedures against the requirements of the standard during the adequacy audit ensures that the organization has considered the mandatory requirements of the standard. Omissions that have not been explained must be clarified before the on-site audit. With the benefit of the preaudit visit, the description of the processes and their interaction is likely to be more readily understood.

The real issue for the audit team is to satisfy itself that the processes are planned and defined and that the controls described appear to be adequate. The high-level checklist and audit planner shown here may be used to complete the adequacy audit (see Figures 5.1 and 5.2).

The Adequacy Audit Checklist Planner is a simple aid that enables the audit team to ensure that each requirement is addressed or excluded as appropriate. Where necessary an auditor can make a note to seek further clarification about an issue prior to the on-site audit. The information received can be used to record the clarification that was given, and a decision can be made about the state of adequacy. If the decision is that the documented system does not meet the standard's requirements, the lead auditor would normally pursue this until a resolution is agreed to.

Adequacy Audit Worksheet			
	Yes	*No*	*Comments*
Has the company clearly defined the scope of the QMS? If yes, state the scope. Does the scope match the stated objectives of your audit?			
Does the scope state exclusions from ISO 9001:2000 requirements? If yes, are the exclusions appropriate?			
Does the company have a documented quality policy?			
Has the company stated its quality objectives?			
Does the company have a quality manual? • Has the company defined the scope of the system? • Are there any exclusions from ISO 9001:2000 requirements? • Does the manual refer to the QMS documented procedures? • Does it define the interaction between the QMS processes?			
Does the company have procedures in place required by ISO 9001:2000? • Document control (4.2.3) • Records (4.2.4) • Internal audit (8.2.2) • Nonconformity (8.3) • Corrective action (8.5.2) • Preventive action (8.5.3)			

(continued)

Figure 5.1 Adequacy Audit Worksheet.

	Yes	No	Comments
Is there evidence that the quality manual and procedures have been approved for adequacy prior to issue?			
Is there evidence that the quality manual and procedures are subject to document control (4.2.3)?			
Is the status of the documents provided clearly defined?			
Does each procedure fully cover the requirements of its relevant ISO clause? (e.g., document control—the requirements of clause 4.2.3)			
Has the company identified its processes?			
Has the company defined methods of managing and controlling its processes?			
Has the company identified the records to be retained? If yes, do they include the records required by the standard?			
Is there a focus on continual improvement?			
Is there a focus on customer satisfaction?			
Have responsibilities and authorities been defined?			
Has a management representative been appointed?			
Do we require further information or a site visit before we can plan our audit?			
What additional information do we require?			

Figure 5.1 Continued.

Adequacy Audit Checklist Planner				
Requirement	*Addressed?*	*Issue to be clarified*	*Clarification*	*Adequate?*
4.1				
4.2.1				
4.2.2				
4.2.3				
4.2.4				
5.1				
5.2				
5.3				
5.4.1				
5.4.2				
5.5.1				

(continued)

Figure 5.2   Adequacy Audit Checklist Planner.

Adequacy Audit Checklist Planner				
Requirement	Addressed?	Issue to be clarified	Clarification	Adequate?
5.5.2				
5.5.3				
5.6.1				
5.6.2				
5.6.3				
6.1				
6.2.1				
6.2.2				
6.3				
6.4				

(continued)

Figure 5.2 Continued.

Adequacy Audit Checklist Planner				
Requirement	*Addressed?*	*Issue to be clarified*	*Clarification*	*Adequate?*
7.1				
7.2.1				
7.2.2				
7.2.3				
7.3.1				
7.3.2				
7.3.3				
7.3.4				
7.3.5				
7.3.6				

(continued)

Figure 5.2   Continued.

Adequacy Audit Checklist Planner				
Requirement	*Addressed?*	*Issue to be clarified*	*Clarification*	*Adequate?*
7.3.7				
7.4.1				
7.4.2				
7.4.3				
7.5.1				
7.5.2				
7.5.3				
7.5.4				
7.5.5				
7.6				

(continued)

Figure 5.2 Continued.

Adequacy Audit Checklist Planner				
Requirement	*Addressed?*	*Issue to be clarified*	*Clarification*	*Adequate?*
8.1				
8.2.1				
8.2.2				
8.2.3				
8.2.4				
8.3				
8.4				
8.5.1				
8.5.2				
8.5.3				

Figure 5.2 Continued.

SUMMARY OF INITIAL PREPARATION

At the end of the initial preparation the following conditions should have been met:

- The scope, exclusions, and objectives are clear
- The reference criteria (for example, standards and contracts) are known
- Key documentation has been obtained (for example, quality manual, procedures, process documents, organizational chart, list of names)
- Auditors have knowledge of the organization's products, processes, layout, location, shift pattern, and security and safety requirements
- Specialist areas are understood
- The auditee understands the protocols involved and has agreed to provide the necessary facilities to the audit team (for example, office, phone, and so on)
- The priorities for the audit have been determined

Finally, any previous audit findings, if they can be obtained, will prove helpful to the audit team.

The audit team is now in a position to begin the detailed planning of the audit—for example, arranging a schedule of interviews, preparing checklists, and agreeing who on the team:

- will speak to whom in the organization;
- about what;
- why;
- at what time; and
- for how long.

CHAPTER 6

Detailed Planning

THE SELECTION OF GUIDES (ESCORTS)

The auditee's management team needs to give serious consideration to the selection of people who will act as the audit team's guides. Ideally the guides will have completed some auditor training. In addition, guides with the following attributes will enable a smooth audit process:

- Knowledge of the organization's products, processes, and personnel
- An ability to explain the quality system
- The authority to accept nonconformities on behalf of the organization

BRIEFING THE AUDIT TEAM

The lead auditor needs to confirm the audit scope and objectives and explain any issues raised by the adequacy audit or the initial preparation. Any information about the organization's culture, background, products, and processes that can be shared among the team will of course be valuable.

The lead auditor and the team members can begin to agree on who is going to do what and the protocols to be followed (for example, when issues need clarification or regarding communication).

UNDERSTANDING THE BENEFITS OF DETAILED PLANNING

Credibility is an important commodity for the audit team to possess, and preparation is a sure way of ensuring that the team has that credibility. The more it knows about the organization and its system the better.

The team has to master five basic skills:

- Ask questions
- Listen to the answers
- Evaluate the answers
- Make decisions
- Manage time

All auditors must remember this word: PREPARATION. Mastery of the skills just listed can be achieved only if adequate time is given to preparation. It is the most important factor to be honored by the audit team.

Auditors need to have a sound tactical approach. That can be achieved only through adequate preparation.

FINAL CONSIDERATIONS OF DETAILED PLANNING

The audit team needs to consider the various forms of objective evidence that it will examine and how it will go about examining it:

- Documents
- Records
- Process methods
- Products
- Essential questions
- Critical people
- Equipment
- Departments
- Results

UNDERSTANDING THE VARIOUS METHODS

A number of methods are open to auditors. They are not right or wrong; they are just different, and the choice of a particular method is determined by the prevailing circumstances (that is, scope, objectives, logistics).

Forward Trace and Backward Trace

Figure 6.1 depicts two audit methods, each of which is designed to follow an audit trail. In a forward trace an auditor might begin with a sales inquiry and follows all the transactions associated with that inquiry through each department of the business until the dispatch note at the delivery element of the process. It is prudent to ensure that the inquiry has been completed before beginning the trail.

A backward trace reverses that process: the auditor might start with a dispatch note and ask to see the related picking list. Then he or she might look for the ship-to-stores note; the final inspection records; the goods inwards records and traceability records; the production schedule; and finally the sales order, order acknowledgment, and inquiry.

Horizontal and Vertical Methods

In a horizontal audit (see Figure 6.2), the auditor focuses on the activities within a given function or department. This typically involves using the procedure or work instructions for a department. The horizontal audit is often the method used in internal audits.

The vertical audit (see Figure 6.2) follows the outputs from one function, department, or process element to the next. This may relate to a contract, product, or project. In this way it is similar to the forward trace audit.

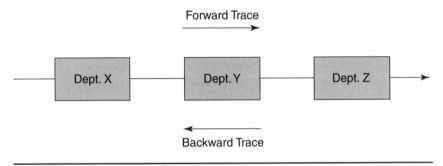

Figure 6.1 Forward trace and backward trace.

Source: Eurospan Developments Ltd. QMS Auditor/Lead Auditor Course 2000, section 11. Used with permission.

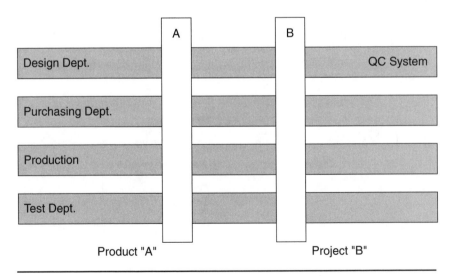

Figure 6.2 Horizontal and vertical audits.

Source: Eurospan Developments Ltd. QMS Auditor/Lead Auditor Course 2000, section 11. Used with permission.

The Process Inputs Method

Using an Ishikawa diagram as a template, auditors can consider the inter-relationship between the traditional process attributes and pertinent requirements of the standard. Using the model in Figure 6.3, auditors can ask sensible questions about any process aligned with the requirements of ISO 9001 (clause numbers shown under the headings of people, proce-dures, product, plant and equipment, performance measures, and place).

The clear emphasis on measures is an interesting and important development and an improvement in the new version of the standard. Link the requirements shown in Figure 6.3 to the following questions and the basis of the audit checklist is commenced:

- What is the purpose of the process?
- What are the process inputs?
- What are the process outputs?
- What are the process controls?
- What resources are required?
- How was the level of resources determined?
- What are the measures of effectiveness, efficiency, and flexibility?

The resource issue is one that auditors need to consider carefully. Additional questions may include these:

- What is the rationale behind the resource plan?
- Is there evidence that the resource planning process is reviewed for effectiveness?
- Has some contingency planning been taken into account?

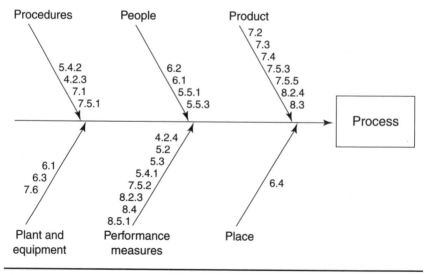

Figure 6.3 The process inputs method and the requirements of ISO 9001:2000.

PLANNING THE RESOURCES REQUIRED FOR THE AUDIT

From initial observation, it is apparent that planning for an audit against the new standard takes longer than it did for the previous version. This is because the new standard requires a much greater understanding of the business and its processes than previously was the case. The focus on measurement and processes rather than documentation is a significant improvement and should enhance the value-adding contribution of the audit process.

A number of factors must be considered when finalizing the number of auditors required in the team:

- Scope
- Objectives
- Number of employees
- Physical size of the organization
- Whether it is a full audit, a follow-up visit, or a surveillance visit
- The complexity of the processes (for example, the need for a specialist)

It is also prudent for lead auditors to remember that they should not plan as intensive a program for themselves as they do for the other members of the team—otherwise, they will leave themselves no capacity to enter into disputes and resolve problems.

THE AUDIT PROGRAM

The lead auditor will finalize the audit program and send it to the auditee's representative. A sample is shown in Figure 6.4.

In such a program, it is clear which auditor will speak to which auditee, about what, and for how long. This style of program is repeated for each day of the audit.

Some negotiation will always take place after the program is finalized, even during the opening meeting. Audit teams must try and be as flexible as possible.

AUDIT CHECKLISTS

There are many different ways of preparing checklists—for example, the tree diagrams discussed in chapter 2 are an effective way of ensuring that all the requirements of the standard are covered.

Day One of Three-Day Audit									
	0900	1000	1100	1200	1300	1400	1500	1600	
Lead auditor	Opening meeting and tour	Management Responsibility T. Chadwick			Lunch	Resources Mel Shaw	Training Bill Dick	Review	
Auditor 1	Opening meeting and tour	Document control Peter Talbot		Records Peter Talbot	Lunch	Product realization John Wadham/ Julian Benton		Review	
Auditor 2	Opening meeting and tour	Internal audit Mike Howard	Customer focus Steve Gregg		Lunch	Purchasing Bob Clarke		Review	

Figure 6.4   A sample audit program.

Another method is the criteria-based checklist, where each requirement of the standard is, in effect, turned into a question. A sample criteria-based checklist designed to audit against ISO 9001:2000 is presented here. The checklist is organized according to the relevant clauses of the standard.

Criteria-Based Checklist for ISO 9001:2000

4.1 General requirements

Verify that the organization has established, documented, implemented, and/or maintained a quality management system.

Verify that the organization has continually improved its effectiveness in accordance with the requirements of this international standard.

Verify that the organization has:

    (a) identified the processes needed for the quality management system and/or their application throughout the organization;

    (b) determined the sequence and interaction of the processes;

(c) determined criteria and methods needed to ensure that both the operation and control of the processes are effective;

(d) ensured the availability of resources and information necessary to support the operation and monitoring of the processes;

(e) monitored, measured, and analyzed the processes; and

(f) implemented actions necessary to achieve planned results and continual improvement of the processes.

Verify that the processes are managed by the organization in accordance with the requirements of the international standard.

Verify that where the organization has chosen to outsource any process that affects product conformity with requirements, the organization has ensured control over such processes.

Verify that control of outsourced processes has been identified within the quality management system.

4.2 Documentation requirements

4.2.1 General

Verify that the quality management system documentation includes:

(a) documented statements of a quality policy and quality objectives;

(b) a quality manual;

(c) documented procedures required by the international standard;

(d) documents needed by the organization to ensure the effective planning, operation, and control of its processes; and

(e) records required by the international standard.

4.2.2 Quality manual

Verify that the organization has established and/or maintained a quality manual that includes:

(a) the scope of the quality management system, including details of and justification for any exclusions;

(b) the documented procedures established for the quality management system, or reference to them; and

(c) a description of the interaction between the processes of the quality management system.

4.2.3 Control of documents

Ensure that documents required by the quality management system are controlled.

Verify that records have been controlled according to the requirements given in ISO 9001:2000 clause 4.2.4.

Examine the documented procedure established to define the controls needed:

(a) to approve documents for adequacy prior to issue;

(b) to review and update as necessary and reapprove documents;

(c) to ensure that changes and the current revision status of documents are identified;

(d) to ensure that relevant versions of applicable documents are available at points of use;

(e) to ensure that documents remain legible and readily identifiable;

(f) to ensure that documents of external origin are identified and their distribution controlled; and

(g) to prevent the unintended use of obsolete documents and apply suitable identification to them if they are retained for any purpose.

4.2.4 Control of records

Ensure that records have been established and maintained to provide evidence of conformity to requirements and of the effective operation of the quality management system.

Verify that records are legible, readily identifiable, and/or retrievable.

Ensure that a documented procedure has been established to define the controls needed for the identification, storage, protection, retrieval, retention time, and/or disposition of records.

5 Management responsibility

5.1 Management commitment

Examine objective evidence that top management has provided evidence of its commitment to the development and implementation of the quality management system and/or continually improving its effectiveness by:

(a) communicating to the organization the importance of meeting customer as well as statutory and regulatory requirements;

(b) establishing the quality policy;

(c) ensuring that quality objectives are established;

(d) conducting management reviews; and

(e) ensuring the availability of resources.

5.2 Customer focus

Verify through objective evidence that top management has ensured that customer requirements are determined and are met with the aim of enhancing customer satisfaction.

5.3 Quality policy

Seek objective evidence that top management has ensured that the quality policy:

(a) is appropriate to the purpose of the organization;
(b) includes a commitment to comply with requirements and continually improve the effectiveness of the quality management system;
(c) provides a framework for establishing and reviewing quality objectives;
(d) is communicated and understood within the organization; and
(e) is reviewed for continuing suitability.

5.4 Planning

5.4.1 Quality objectives

Examine objective evidence that top management has ensured that quality objectives, including those needed to meet requirements for product, have been established at relevant functions and levels in the organization.

Ensure that the quality objectives are measurable and/or consistent with the quality policy.

5.4.2 Quality management system planning

Verify that top management has ensured that:

(a) the planning of the quality management system is carried out in order to meet the requirements given in ISO 9001:2000 clause 4.1 and/or the quality objectives; and
(b) the integrity of the quality management system is maintained when changes to the quality management system are planned and implemented.

5.5 Responsibility, authority, and communication

5.5.1 Responsibility and authority

Examine evidence that shows that top management has ensured that responsibilities and authorities are defined and communicated within the organization.

5.5.2 Management representative

Verify that top management has appointed a member of management who, irrespective of other responsibilities, has responsibility and authority that includes:

(a) ensuring that processes needed for the quality management system are established, implemented, and maintained;
(b) reporting to top management on the performance of the quality management system and any need for improvement; and
(c) ensuring the promotion of awareness of customer requirements throughout the organization.

5.5.3 Internal communication

Seek evidence that illustrates that top management has ensured that appropriate communications processes are established in the organization and/or that communication takes place regarding the effectiveness of the quality management system.

5.6 Management review

5.6.1 General

Look at the evidence that demonstrates that top management has reviewed the organization's quality management system, at planned intervals, to ensure its continuing suitability, adequacy, and effectiveness.

Ensure that the review does include assessing opportunities for improvement and/or the need for changes to the quality management system, including the quality policy and quality objectives.

Examine the records from management reviews.

5.6.2 Review input

Ensure that the input to management review includes information on:

(a) results of audits;
(b) customer feedback;
(c) process performance and product conformity;
(d) status of preventive and corrective actions;
(e) follow-up actions from previous management reviews;
(f) changes that could affect the quality management system; and
(g) recommendations for improvement.

5.6.3 Review output

Ensure that the output from the management review includes any decisions and actions related to:

(a) improvement of the effectiveness of the quality management system and its processes;

(b) improvement of product related to customer requirements; and

(c) resource needs.

6 Resource management

6.1 Provision of resources

Verify that the organization has determined and/or provided the resources needed to:

(a) implement and maintain the quality management system and continually improve its effectiveness; and

(b) enhance customer satisfaction by meeting customer requirements.

6.2 Human resources

6.2.1 General

Ensure that the organization can demonstrate that personnel performing work affecting product quality are competent on the basis of appropriate education, training, skills, and experience.

6.2.2 Competence, awareness, and training

Look for evidence to demonstrate that the organization has:

(a) determined the necessary competence for personnel performing work affecting product quality;

(b) provided training or taken other actions to satisfy those needs;

(c) evaluated the effectiveness of the actions taken;

(d) ensured that its personnel are aware of the relevance and importance of their activities and how they contribute to the achievement of the quality objectives; and

(e) maintained appropriate records of education, training, skills, and experience.

6.3 Infrastructure

Verify that the organization has determined, provided, and/or maintained the infrastructure needed to achieve conformity to product requirements. (See ISO 9001:2000 clause 6.3 for characteristics included under the heading "Infrastructure.")

6.4 Work environment

Ensure that the organization has determined and managed the work environment needed to achieve conformity to product requirements.

7 Product realization

7.1 Planning of product realization

Examine evidence to show that the organization has planned and developed the processes needed for product realization.

Ensure that planning of product realization is consistent with the requirements of the other processes of the quality management system.

Verify that in planning product realization, the organization has determined the following, as appropriate:

(a) quality objectives and requirements for the product;
(b) the need to establish processes and documents and provide resources specific to the product;
(c) required verification, validation, monitoring, inspection, and test activities specific to the product and the criteria for product acceptance; and
(d) records needed to provide evidence that the realization processes and resulting product meet requirements.

Look at the output of the planning of product realization and verify that it is in a form suitable for the organization's method of operations.

7.2 Customer-related processes

7.2.1 Determination of requirements related to the product

Examine how the organization has determined:

(a) requirements specified by the customer, including the requirements for delivery and postdelivery activities;
(b) requirements not stated by the customer but necessary for specified or intended use, where known;
(c) statutory and regulatory requirements related to the product; and
(d) any additional requirements determined by the organization.

7.2.2 Review of requirements related to the product

Look for evidence that the organization has reviewed the requirements related to the product.

Ensure that the review of product requirements has been conducted prior to the organization's commitment to supply a product to the customer.

Look at how the organization has ensured that:

(a) product requirements are defined;
(b) contract or order requirements differing from those previously expressed are resolved; and
(c) the organization has the ability to meet the defined requirements.

Examine records of the results of the review and verify that actions arising from the review have been taken.

Where the customer provides no documented statement of requirement, clarify how the customer requirements have been confirmed by the organization before acceptance.

Where product requirements are changed, clarify how the organization has ensured that relevant documents are amended and/or that relevant personnel are made aware of the changed requirements.

7.2.3 Customer communication

Clarify how the organization has determined and/or implemented effective arrangements for communicating with customers in relation to:

(a) product information;
(b) enquiries, contracts, or order handling, including amendments; and
(c) customer feedback, including customer complaints.

7.3 Design and development

7.3.1 Design and development planning

Verify that the organization has planned and/or controlled the design and development of product.

During the design and development planning, check how the organization has determined:

(a) the design and development stages;
(b) the review, verification, and validation that are appropriate to each design and development stage; and
(c) the responsibilities and authorities for design and development.

Check how the organization has managed the interfaces between different groups involved in design and development to ensure effective communication and/or clear assignment of responsibility.

Clarify how planning output has been updated, as appropriate, as the design and development progresses.

7.3.2 Design and development inputs

Examine how inputs relating to product requirements have been determined and/or records maintained.

Ensure that design and development inputs include:

(a) functional and performance requirements;
(b) applicable statutory and regulatory requirements;
(c) where applicable, information derived from previous similar designs; and
(d) other requirements essential for design and development.

Look for evidence that design and development inputs are reviewed for adequacy.

Verify that design and development requirements are complete, unambiguous, and/or not in conflict with each other.

7.3.3 Design and development outputs

Ensure that the outputs of design and development are provided in a form that enables verification against the design and development input and are approved prior to release.

Verify that design and development outputs:

(a) meet the input requirements for design and development;
(b) provide appropriate information for purchasing, production, and for service provision;
(c) contain or reference product acceptance criteria; and
(d) specify the characteristics of the product that are essential for its safe and proper use.

7.3.4 Design and development review

Examine how at suitable stages, systematic reviews of design and development are performed in accordance with planned arrangements:

(a) to evaluate the ability of the results of design and development to meet requirements; and
(b) to identify any problems and propose necessary actions.

Check that participants in design and development reviews do include representatives of functions concerned with the design and development stage(s) being reviewed.

Examine records of the results of the design and development reviews and/or any necessary actions.

7.3.5 Design and development verification

Ensure that verification is performed in accordance with planned arrangements to ensure that the design and development outputs have met the design and development input requirements.

Check the records of the results of the verification and any necessary actions.

7.3.6 Design and development validation

Explore how design and development validation is performed in accordance with planned arrangements to ensure that the resulting product is capable of meeting the requirements for the specified application or intended use, where known.

Clarify that wherever practicable, validation is completed prior to the delivery or implementation of the product.

Examine records of the results of validation and any necessary actions.

7.3.7 Control of design and development changes

Verify that design and development changes are identified and/or records maintained.

Seek evidence to show that design changes are reviewed, verified, and/or validated, as appropriate, and/or approved before implementation.

Clarify how the review of design and development changes includes evaluation of the effect of the changes on constituent parts and product already delivered.

Examine records of the results of the review of changes and any necessary actions.

7.4 Purchasing

7.4.1 Purchasing process

Check how the organization has ensured that purchased product conforms to specified purchase requirements.

Verify that the type and extent of control applied to the supplier and the purchased product is dependent upon the effect of the purchased product on subsequent product realization or the final product.

Look for evidence that the organization has evaluated and/or selected suppliers based on their ability to supply product in accordance with the organization's requirements.

Examine the criteria for selection, evaluation, and reevaluation of suppliers.

Examine records of the results of evaluations and any necessary actions arising from the evaluation.

7.4.2 Purchasing information

Check that purchasing information describes the product to be purchased, including where appropriate:

(a) requirements for approval of product, procedures, processes, and equipment;
(b) requirements for qualification of personnel; and
(c) quality management system requirements.

Understand how the organization ensures the adequacy of specified purchase requirements prior to their communication to the supplier.

7.4.3 Verification of purchased product

Clarify how the organization establishes and implements the inspection or other activities necessary for ensuring that purchased product meets specified purchase requirements.

Where the organization or its customer intends to perform verification at the supplier's premises, check that the organization has stated the intended verification arrangements and/or method of product release in the purchasing information.

7.5 Production and service provision

7.5.1 Control of production and service provision

Verify that the organization plans and carries out production and service provision under controlled conditions.

Verify that controlled conditions include, as applicable:

(a) the availability of information that describes the characteristics of the product;
(b) the availability of work instructions, as necessary;
(c) the use of suitable equipment;
(d) the availability and use of monitoring and measuring devices;
(e) the implementation of monitoring and measurement; and
(f) the implementation of release, delivery, and postdelivery activities.

7.5.2 Validation of processes for production and service provision

Ensure that the organization validates any processes for production and service provision where the resulting output cannot be verified by subsequent monitoring or measurement.

Clarify how validation of processes demonstrates the ability of such processes to achieve planned results.

Verify that the organization establishes arrangements for such processes including, as applicable:

(a) defined criteria for review and approval of the processes;
(b) approval of equipment and qualification of personnel;
(c) use of specific methods and procedures;
(d) requirements for records; and
(e) revalidation.

7.5.3 Identification and traceability

Check that, where appropriate, the organization identifies the product by suitable means throughout product realization.

Ensure that the organization identifies the product status with respect to monitoring and measurement requirements.

Where traceability is a requirement, clarify how the organization controls and records the unique identification of the product.

7.5.4 Customer property

Understand how the organization exercises care with customer property while it is under the organization's control or being used by the organization.

How does the organization identify, verify, protect, and/or safeguard customer property provided for use or incorporation into the product?

Where customer property is lost, damaged, or otherwise found to be unsuitable for use, how is this reported to the customer and/or records maintained?

7.5.5 Preservation of product

Based on the pertinent contractual and legislative requirements, how does the organization preserve the conformity of product during internal processing and delivery to the intended destination?

Ensure that this preservation includes identification, handling, packaging, storage, and protection.

Ensure that preservation applies to the constituent parts of a product.

7.6 Control of monitoring and measuring devices

How does the organization determine the monitoring and measurement to be undertaken and the monitoring and/or measuring devices needed to provide evidence of conformity of product to determined requirements?

Does the organization establish processes to ensure that monitoring and measurement can be carried out and/or are carried out in a manner that is consistent with the monitoring and measurement requirements?

Where necessary to ensure valid results, is measuring equipment:

(a) Calibrated or verified at specified intervals, or prior to use, against measurement standards traceable to international or national measurement standards? Where no such standards exist, what is the basis used for calibration or verification, and is this recorded?
(b) Adjusted or readjusted as necessary?
(c) Identified to enable the calibration status to be determined?
(d) Safeguarded from adjustments that would invalidate the measurement result?
(e) Protected from damage and deterioration during handling, maintenance, and storage?

Clarify how the organization assesses and/or records the validity of the previous measuring results when the equipment is found not to conform to requirements.

Verify that the organization takes appropriate action on the equipment and any product affected when the equipment is found not to conform to requirements.

Examine records of the results of calibration and verification.

When used in the monitoring and measurement of specified requirements, how is the ability of computer software to satisfy the intended application confirmed?

Clarify how the ability of computer software to satisfy the intended application is confirmed prior to initial use and reconfirmed as necessary.

8 Measurement, analysis, and improvement

8.1 General

How does the organization plan and implement the monitoring, measurement, analysis, and improvement processes needed:

(a) to demonstrate conformity of the product?
(b) to ensure conformity of the quality management system?
(c) to continually improve the effectiveness of the quality management system?

Ensure that monitoring, measurement, analysis, and improvement processes include determination of applicable methods, including statistical techniques, and the extent of their use.

8.2 Monitoring and measurement

8.2.1 Customer satisfaction

As one of the measurements of the performance of the quality management system, how does the organization monitor information relating to customer perception as to whether the organization has met customer requirements?

Explore the methods used for obtaining and using this information.

8.2.2 Internal audit

Verify that the organization conducts internal audits at planned intervals to determine whether the quality management system:

(a) conforms to the planned arrangements and/or to the requirements of ISO 9001:2000 and/or to the quality management system requirements established by the organization; and
(b) is effectively implemented and maintained.

Is the audit program planned taking into consideration the status and importance of the processes and areas to be audited, as well as the results of previous audits?

Are the audit criteria, scope, frequency, and/or methods defined?

Verify that the selection of auditors and conduct of audits ensures objectivity and impartiality of the audit process.

Verify that auditors do not audit their own work.

Are the responsibilities and requirements for planning and conducting audits and for reporting results and/or maintaining records defined in a documented procedure?

Look for evidence that the management responsible for the area being audited ensures that actions are taken without undue delay to eliminate detected nonconformities and their causes.

Examine the follow-up activities. Do they include the verification of the actions taken and the reporting of verification results?

8.2.3 Monitoring and measurement of processes

Clarify how the organization applies suitable methods for monitoring and, where applicable, measurement of the quality management system processes.

Verify that the methods for monitoring and, where applicable, measurement of the quality management system processes demonstrate the ability of the processes to achieve planned results.

When planned results are not achieved, is corrective action taken, as appropriate, to ensure conformity of the product?

8.2.4 Monitoring and measurement of product

Verify that the organization monitors and measures the characteristics of the product to verify that product requirements have been met.

Clarify how monitoring and measuring of the characteristics of the product to verify that product requirements have been met is carried out at appropriate stages of the product realization process in accordance with the planned arrangements.

What evidence of conformity with the acceptance criteria is maintained?

Do records indicate the person(s) authorizing release of product?

Ensure that product release and service delivery does not proceed before the planned arrangements have been satisfactorily completed. Is there evidence of approval by a relevant authority and, where applicable, by the customer?

8.3 Control of nonconforming product

Verify that the organization ensures that product that does not conform to product requirements is identified and controlled to prevent its unintended use or delivery.

What are the controls and related responsibilities and authorities for dealing with nonconforming product? Are these defined in a documented procedure?

Verify that the organization deals with nonconforming product by one or more of the following ways:

(a) By taking action to eliminate the detected nonconformity
(b) By authorizing its use, release, or acceptance under concession by a relevant authority and, where applicable, by the customer
(c) By taking action to preclude its original intended use or application

Examine the records of the nature of nonconformities and any subsequent actions taken, including concessions obtained.

Ensure that when nonconforming product is corrected it is subject to reverification to demonstrate conformity to the requirements.

When nonconforming product is detected after delivery or use has started, how does the organization take action appropriate to the effects, or potential effects, of the nonconformity?

8.4 Analysis of data

Understand how the organization determines, collects, and/or analyzes appropriate data to demonstrate the suitability and effectiveness of the quality management system and to evaluate where continual improvement of the effectiveness of the quality management system can be made.

Clarify how data to demonstrate the suitability and effectiveness of the quality management system and to evaluate where continual improvement of the effectiveness of the quality management system can be made include data generated as a result of monitoring and measurement and from other relevant sources.

Does the analysis of data provide information relating to:

(a) customer satisfaction;
(b) conformity to product requirements;
(c) characteristics and trends of processes and products including opportunities for preventive action; and
(d) suppliers.

8.5 Improvement

8.5.1 Continual improvement

How does the organization continually improve the effectiveness of the quality management system through the use of the quality policy, quality objectives, audit results, analysis of data, corrective and preventive actions, and/or management review?

8.5.2 Corrective action

Does the organization take action to eliminate the cause of nonconformities in order to prevent recurrence?

Are corrective actions appropriate to the effects of the nonconformities encountered?

Does the documented procedure define requirements for:

(a) reviewing nonconformities (including customer complaints)?
(b) determining the causes of nonconformities?
(c) evaluating the need for action to ensure that nonconformities do not recur?
(d) determining and implementing action needed?
(e) records of the results of action taken?
(f) reviewing corrective action taken?

8.5.3 Preventive action

Examine how the organization determines action to eliminate the causes of potential nonconformities in order to prevent their occurrence.

Are preventive actions appropriate to the effects of the potential problems?

Does the documented procedure define requirements for:

(a) determining potential nonconformities and their causes?
(b) evaluating the need for action to prevent occurrence of noncon-
     formities?
(c) determining and implementing action needed?
(d) records of results of action taken?
(e) reviewing preventive action taken?

Other Forms of Checklists

Another variation of the checklist is the departmental type, which may be
prepared for any function or process within the organization.

Figure 6.5 is a departmental type and shows an auditor probing from
business objectives to specific departmental activities.

Figure 6.6 shows an auditor probing a core business process (new
product introduction). Following from understanding the rationale of the
decision to accept a new product enquiry to the definition of responsibilities associated with the process of introducing the new product.

Figure 6.7 shows how an auditor might design questions around the
simple process model of inputs, outputs, resources, and controls.

Figure 6.8 relates to more generic questions associated with a core
business process.

(Note that NCR in these checklists stands for nonconformity report.)

Summary of Checklists

What is clear is that checklists are very personal things. They often combine criteria-based, process, function, and general questions.

Often when asking the auditee questions, the auditor does not use the
exact wording of the question as written. The wording is determined
more by the circumstances and the responsiveness of the auditee.

One thing is sure: the second question in an audit is determined by
the answer to the first question and not by the next question on the checklist. While checklists may be good aide memoirs, ensuring depth and continuity, care must be taken to ensure that they do not stifle originality.

Much debate has occurred about whether the auditor should send the
questionnaire to the auditee in advance. Consider this: If you knew all the
exam questions before you sat down to take it, do you think you would fail?

No.	Ref.	Question	Finding	NCR	Comments
		Audit Checklist Example 1			
		Audit no.: 1 Location: XYZ Company, Commercial Sales Date: 2/3/01			
		Auditor: J. Bull Auditee: Amanda Heath			
1	7.2.1	How does the organization capture the requirements of customers?			
2	7.2.1	Can you show me, for contract number 68, that the organization considered statutory and regulatory requirements?			
3	7.2.1	In your customer management process, you refer to information regarding product standards. How is this information communicated to sales and engineering personnel?			
4	7.2.3	How do you use feedback from your customer, including customer complaints to refine the customer management process?			
5	8.2.1	How does the organization monitor information relating to customer perception of service performance levels?			
6	8.2.1	How is customer perception data analyzed and prioritized for action?			

Figure 6.5 Departmental type of questions.

No.	Ref.	Question	Finding	NCR	Comments
		Audit Checklist Example 2			
		Audit no.: 1 Location: XYZ Company, New Product Development Process Date: 2/3/01			
		Auditor: J. Bull Auditee: J. Benton			
1	8.4	How are management decisions regarding new product development influenced by customer and market intelligence?			
2	8.5.3	During new product development, how does the organization identify risks and constraints?			
3	5.6.3	Following management reviews, how are objectives and targets set for improvement of product related to customer requirements? And what is the process by which these are agreed on for new product development projects?			
4	7.3.1	How are responsibilities defined and activities prioritized for the project team members?			
5	7.3.1	How does the organization ensure that adequate resources are provided to new product introduction teams? And that			
	6.2.2	the competence of project team members is appropriate for the work to be undertaken?			

Figure 6.6 Questions for a core business process.

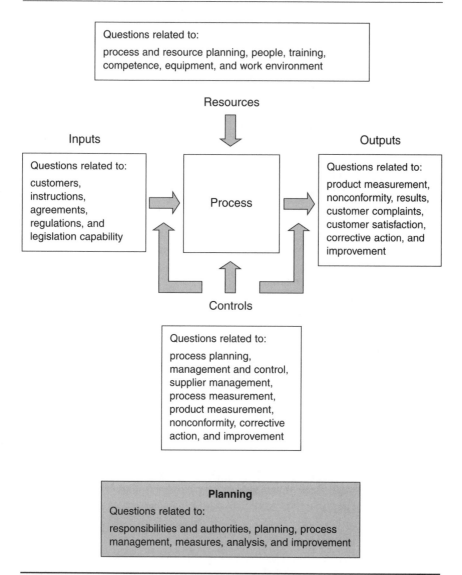

Figure 6.7 Questions based on the simple process model.

Audit no.: 1 Location: XYZ Company, Business Process Management Date: 3/2/01					
Auditor: J. Bull			Auditee: T. Chadwick		
No.	**Ref.**	**Question**	**Finding**	**NCR**	**Comments**
1		*Ask for an overview of the process approach.*			
2	*4.1.b*	*How are process interrelationships identified, managed, resolved, and improved?*			
3	*4.1.c*	*How are processes controlled? (For example, procedures, specifications.)*			
4	*5.4.1*	*Are there any quality objectives related to the specific process?*			
5	*8.1*	*How is achievement of objectives measured?*			
6	*8.2.3*	*How are processes measured?*			
7	*8.2.3/4*	*Examine process and product monitoring results to determine if requirements are met.*			

Figure 6.8   Generic process questions.

In preparing any type of checklist one follows a logical process:

- Read and understand the applicable documentation (for example, manual, standard, procedures, contract)
- In the context of the audit scope and objectives, determine the priorities
- Determine what it is you wish to know
- Develop a question that will give you that information

Questions should be short, focused, and follow a logical sequence; they should not jump around from the start of a procedure to the end and then into the middle. This confuses the auditee.

Although the auditor is using the checklist to ensure comprehensive coverage of the areas to be investigated, he or she must apply a reality check—that is, "Can we ask this many questions in the time available?" Too many auditors write too many questions. Questions must be simple, and irrespective of what is actually written on the checklist, they must be asked in the language of the auditee. Bad auditors ask questions that are too long and worded around the numbers and phrases of the standard.

The checklist is a road map not a railway track: it can be set aside temporarily if something worth pursuing is highlighted.

Finally, remember that during the closing meeting and the report writing it is imperative that the auditor can trace back to a finding. The checklist should provide a vehicle to link the:

- question number;
- clause or requirement number;
- question asked;
- answer received, including all references (for example, record numbers, dates, people's names, equipment number, machine number, product batch numbers); and
- decision made (conformity/nonconformity, effective/ineffective, strength or area for improvement).

CHAPTER 7

The Human Side of Auditing

WHY THIS CHAPTER IS NECESSARY

It is sad but true that too many auditors have become mechanistic in their approach. They have learned the requirements of the ISO standard by heart and have been asking the same type of questions of the same type of people and getting the same type of answers for longer than they care to remember. As a result, they have lost the capacity to master the five basic skills:

- Ask questions
- Listen to the answers
- Evaluate the answers
- Make decisions
- Manage time

The greatest of these shortcomings is the loss of a willingness or capacity to listen to answers and then evaluate those answers prior to making a decision. There is a human side to auditing, and adapting the correct personal approach is far more effective than being a clinical investigator.

GETTING TO THE REAL ISSUES

The questions written on the checklist must now be asked of an auditee—often a nervous auditee. The anxiety is not always caused by the auditor; it often is caused by the managers in the auditee's organization. They may have told the auditees: "Don't volunteer any information; don't answer questions that you have not been asked; don't give the auditors anything that they don't ask for—or else!" It is no wonder that auditees are nervous; they are expecting some ogre to confront them.

The auditor must allow the auditee to settle down. The auditor will move from informal "getting-to-know-you" questions to a more structured interview, but the auditee must never feel that he or she is being interrogated.

Softening the questions by using real words rather than the jargon of the standard is important. Alternating the lead-in of the question is also helpful—for example:

What . . .

Why . . .

Where . . .

When . . .

Who . . .

How . . .

But for auditors, getting to the real issues is a function of the follow-on question "Show me." This is not a matter of disbelief or mistrust; it is the auditor's role to satisfy him- or herself that objective evidence exists to demonstrate conformity with the specified requirements.

THE MODERN APPROACH

Good auditors put people at ease, asking questions such as "How long have you worked here?" They adopt a tone of voice that, while inquisitive, is not intimidating. The aggressive auditor is often employing a defensive mechanism to cover up insecurity. There is no justification for an auditor acting in an aggressive manner. It is unprofessional.

The modern approach tends to focus as much on why things are done as on how. In this way auditors use hypothetical questions—the what-if questions—to explore the robustness of the process.

Knowing the information they seek, good auditors are not distracted by long-winded or evasive answers. They are comfortable repeating questions and persisting firmly to resolve issues.

An underused skill of the modern approach is the silent question. The auditor says nothing and just waits. Uncomfortable with the silence, the auditee answers the question that was never asked, and the auditor follows on with a supplementary question. This approach is often highly revealing. (Perhaps this is why managers tell their people never to volunteer information!)

GETTING TO THE RIGHT PEOPLE

It is important that auditors spend an appropriate amount of time with managers. This enables them to form an understanding of the rationale behind approaches and of the level of commitment to the implementation of the system.

Good sense suggests that during the detailed planning, the opening meeting, and even at the start of each interview, the auditor should ensure that the auditee is the right person to be talking to (job titles can be very misleading). Auditees assume that auditors are experts, and, therefore, when an auditor asks an auditee a question, the auditee assumes he or she should know the answer and instead of saying, "I don't know," answers to the best of his or her ability—and that answer may be wrong. The bad auditor immediately records a nonconformity. The good auditor would not be asking the question of the wrong person in the first place.

Managers are skilled at dealing with auditors, and although they speak when asked a question, they too often do not actually say anything; rather they seek to blind the auditor with science or detail or explanations of what is going to be done in the future. Protocol dictates that auditors begin with the managers, even if it is only to say, "Good morning." But the truth, or more appropriately, reality, is in the mouths and hands of those doing the job. They may not be as skilled as the managers in providing politically correct answers. So auditors need to get to the troops and talk to them. The generals may know the plan, but they often are a long way from the trenches.

If auditors do get to the troops, it is important for them to avoid quoting clause numbers or ISO 9001 jargon. They should use terms with which the auditees are familiar, repeat questions, rephrase questions, and clarify why questions are being asked. In a noisy environment, it is often necessary to repeat questions.

If things are good (based on a sample), the auditor should say so and be complimentary. A system that is in conformity and effective is something to be celebrated; it is not, as many auditors think, something to be disappointed about.

Pitching the questions correctly is important, but aiming the questions correctly is even more important. Too many auditors make the mistake of asking the company's managing director about document control or a shop floor operator about the formulation of the quality policy. In the case of the managing director, there will be slight irritation, and in the case of the operator, bewilderment.

OVERENTHUSIASTIC ESCORTS

Sadly, the worst escorts during an audit are the quality professionals or the management representatives who designed the system. They may have spent the last year or two writing procedures, getting commitment from senior managers, and implementing the system, and now the auditor is approaching the one person in the company who is going to say or do all the wrong things. Anxiety gets the better of the escort, and every time a question is asked of the auditee, the escort jumps in to answer. The escort cannot help it, but the auditor has got to stop it and remind the escort of the rules of the game. The escort is there to:

- make the introductions and explain what the auditor is doing;
- ensure that the auditor is talking to the right person;
- clarify any issues that may not be understood by either party; and
- agree to findings.

The escort's role is an important one, and interfering escorts must be reminded of that if they cross the line.

Sometimes escorts wander off and leave the auditor alone; the temptation to begin looking at documents or in files is to be resisted. The good auditor will wait a little while, and if the interval is unacceptably long, he or she will seek to reestablish contact with the management representative and get the escort back or a new escort. Some reassurance should be sought that this event will not be repeated, and a note should be made of the incident in case other members of the team are suffering the same fate.

SAMPLING EVIDENCE

Sampling of documents, records, and products can be done very scientifically using sampling tables, but that seems a little over the top. Whatever method is used to sample, there are risks involved, such as the following:

- The sample is too small
- The sample is not representative
- The sample indicates something is good when it is actually bad
- The sample indicates something is very bad when it is actually generally good

The rules of sampling are clear:

- Determine an appropriate sample size during the detailed planning phase of the audit. This can be based on the known frequency of transactions, or it can be a simple decision to look at 5 or 10 pieces of evidence.
- Look at the specified number of samples, neither less nor more, unless there is a very good reason to change. Looking for extra samples when nothing is wrong suggests to the auditee that the auditor is desperate to find a nonconformity.
- Select your own samples to avoid bias.

Most auditees cannot understand how auditors have the special gift of always asking for that one missing record or that one piece of equipment that is not calibrated. The truth can now be revealed: it is because of the patron saint of auditors, St. Murphy. The following prayer should be recited before all audits:

Dear Patron Saint of Auditors,
Let it be that if it has gone wrong,
Even if it was only once,
That I should find it,
But give me the grace not to smile!

With the rules of sampling and the prayer, auditors need never be anxious about the effectiveness of their samples.

WHAT MAKES A GOOD AUDITOR?

For those of us who aspire to being a good auditor, the list of desirable attributes is long, and can be frustrating to attain:

Personable
Inquisitive
Systems oriented
Objective
Good planner
Problem (not solution) directed
Good researcher
Good speaker and writer
Able to cope with people
Able to ask questions
Constructive
Good listener
Able to prioritize
Resilient
Diplomatic
Self-disciplined
Honest

Patient

Articulate

Industrious

Professional

Interested

Analytical

Unafraid of unpopularity

Human

WHAT MAKES A BAD AUDITOR?

The list of qualities that make for bad auditing can be just as long, but the auditor who knows his or her weaknesses can start to improve:

Argumentative

Undisciplined

Dishonest

Full of opinions

Has closed ears

Impatient

Poor communicator

Lacks energy

Fails to build a good relationship

Unprofessional

Appears uninterested

Accepts things at face value

Wants to be loved!

A QUESTION OF ETHICS

Without a doubt the moral fiber and character of an auditor must be beyond reproach. The behavior of audit teams must be seen as appropriate and professional. There is a risk, within some cultures, that financial or other types of persuasion might be offered to influence decisions. If the team suspects such an offer has been made, it must make sure it has heard correctly what is being proposed and then make equally clear that such approaches are unacceptable. Those commissioning the audit may be interested to know of such approaches. Great care is required—it is a brave auditor who will declare such approaches without a supporting witness. Such is the nature of "misunderstandings."

To avoid such difficulties, auditors need to act honorably (see the International Register of Certificated Auditors and the International Auditor and Training Certification Association codes of conduct). That may include declaring conflicts of interest, respecting confidentiality, and not compromising themselves, the organization they represent, or the auditee. In the event of complaints, it is essential that the auditor cooperates with any investigation—a further reason for keeping good and accurate notes.

It is in the interest of all auditors for those who represent the audit process to conduct themselves in a professional and trustworthy manner. Auditors must take care not to fall prey to their own prejudices or prejudgments. Good auditors enter with an open mind and base all findings on the evidence.

THINGS THAT CAN GO WRONG, ETHICALLY SPEAKING

Sometimes an auditor will uncover unethical practices. For example, the auditor may discover that the organization is engaged in one or more of the following activities. In any of the following cases, it is imperative that the auditor does not compromise himself or herself. Immediate reference should be made to the person(s) who commissioned the audit.

- Discriminating against certain individuals
- Using child labor
- Contaminating the environment
- Trading with governments against which there are trade bans
- Dealing with oppressive regimes
- Making unproven claims for its products
- Involved in the production of pornographic materials
- Involved in the exploitation of the poor and oppressed
- Involved in cruelty to animals
- Producing products that have an adverse effect on health
- Trying to bribe the audit team

CHAPTER 8

The Opening Meeting

WHY THE OPENING MEETING IS NECESSARY

The majority of opening meetings proceed without any complications. This is especially true when all the initial preparation and detailed planning has been completed professionally. The success of the opening meeting is greatly enhanced if the auditors have made a preaudit visit or if the two parties already know each other.

During this meeting the following agenda is covered:

- Make introductions
- Define the purpose
- Finalize program and administrative arrangements
- Confirm the process for feedback of results
- Fix the time and attendees for the closing meeting
- Address any questions

The opening meeting is a vehicle for clarifying and verifying issues that, in truth, should already be understood by both parties.

PREPARING FOR THE OPENING MEETING

It makes sense for the auditor to use the following checklist when preparing for the opening meeting:

- Gather the documentation required.
  - Checklists
  - Attendance register
  - Business cards
  - Notepaper
  - Agenda for the meeting
  - Program for the audit
  - The standard
  - The company's quality system documentation

- Correspondence between the two parties (especially related to scope and objectives)
- Presentation material
- Previous audit reports and nonconformity reports
- Contract documentation
- Organizational chart and list of names
- Ensure that you have a good understanding of the auditee's organization (for example, by reading financial reports, visiting the company Web site, watching company videos). Once again the best preparation is the preaudit visit.
- Confirm the audit 24 hours beforehand.

ARRIVING FOR THE MEETING

Auditors need to remember that this is a meeting, and therefore the normal protocols of meetings apply. An agenda must be prepared, roles and responsibilities must be clarified, and the meeting must be subject to good time management.

The audit team should arrive in good time, and the members should familiarize themselves with the layout of the meeting room. Where practical, the audit team should sit together.

Be prepared to accept business cards from several people, but when the group finally sits down repeat the names of all involved and note them on a piece of paper in front of you corresponding to where people are sitting.

THE INTRODUCTIONS

Thank the hosts for inviting the audit team to come on site and assure them of the best efforts of the team. Explain the process thus far (for example, adequacy audit, preaudit visit).

It is important that everyone involved has the chance to introduce himself or herself and explain his or her role in the audit or responsibility in the organization. Sometimes, the auditees invite observers—for example, their consultant—and it is particularly important in such cases that the ground rules of involvement are clarified. The audit team may have some observers, too—for example, trainee auditors—and their role should be explained. The lead auditor should explain that according to normal protocol the lead auditor chairs the meeting and confirm that this is acceptable to the senior manager.

Explain that this is a short meeting!

THE PURPOSE

The lead auditor should confirm the scope and objectives of the audit and reaffirm the assurance of confidentiality of the audit findings. Clarification of the standard or contract documentation is sensible as some of the auditee's managers may have been invited just to make an impressive show. As the interval between the application for the audit and the day of the opening meeting can be several weeks, or in the worst case several months, it is also a good idea to confirm the status of the quality system documentation.

WORKING THROUGH THE PROGRAM AND CONFIRMING ADMINISTRATIVE ARRANGEMENTS

However much preparation has taken place, the auditee almost inevitably asks to make some changes to the audit program during the opening meeting. Acquiescing to this does not compromise the scope and objectives of the audit; the audit team should seek to be as flexible as possible. Do not accept changes without understanding the reason for the request.

As topics are discussed make sure that the relevant auditor makes eye contact with the relevant manager or escort.

Discuss administrative arrangements, especially issues such as lunches (they should not be too long). Confirm that the team has a meeting room and access to the facilities required (for example, phone, fax, copier).

Discuss the possibility of using a camera to photograph and capture pertinent incidents (for example, leaking pipes or damaged product).

If the audit team has planned to come back on the night shift or early-morning shift, it is important to understand who the contact people are and what additional security, safety, or other arrangements need to be made.

In addition, confirm the auditors' access to the necessary areas and records. There should be no surprises regarding areas or records that are suddenly not going to be available.

THE FEEDBACK OF RESULTS

The escorts' role should be confirmed, and the auditee's most senior manager should give acceptance of the rules specified by the lead auditor.

Time should be taken to explain what will happen *if*, not *when*, a nonconformity is discovered. In longer audits, in addition to securing the immediate agreement of the escort or local manager with regard to a nonconformity, auditors may need to have a daily summary meeting with the management representative. In addition, the lead auditor should explain the different classifications of nonconformities and the consequences of each.

FIXING THE TIME AND ATTENDEES FOR THE CLOSING MEETING

The next time the audit team will see the attendees of the opening meeting together is probably going to be at the closing meeting. It makes sense to fix the time of that meeting as well as its duration and purpose. (Its purpose is to advise the organization of the team's findings and recommendations—there will be no certificates issued!)

Explain that it is not necessary for managers to travel long distances from other sites to be present at this meeting, unless the organization or they themselves decide they must attend.

HANDLING QUESTIONS

At the opening meeting questions about the audit process should be addressed, but questions about interpretation of the standard should not. The auditee's senior managers typically want to know what they have to do during the audit, so a quick run through the following list will help define expectations. Top management must:

- provide evidence of involvement in the design and implementation of the quality system (for example, definition of policy and objectives) and management of the business in a manner that is consistent with the quality principle of leadership;
- provide access to records relating to management review;
- be accessible during the audit to participate in interviews, participate in daily meetings if these have been deemed necessary, and resolve problems should they arise; and
- be available for the opening and closing meetings.

THINGS THAT CAN GO WRONG

As mentioned, the majority of opening meetings take place without incident, but occasionally things do go wrong. Here is a list of potential problems to think about so that you can consider your contingency (they are all from the experience of the author):

- The meeting starts late
- Key auditees do not show up
- Everyone in the company shows up
- You are asked not to audit an area because the company knows it has problems
- You are asked to change the scope
- You are told that you are not welcome
- Someone attempts to bribe you
- Someone has a heart attack during the meeting
- The quality system has been completely rewritten
- The company has a serious industrial dispute
- There are numerous interruptions
- When the audit team enters the room, the management team is having a blazing row
- The company wants to turn a two-day audit into a one-day audit because the factory is going to be closed the next day
- The receivers have been called in
- The company objects to one of the team members

Now, we bet that you are glad that most opening meetings go ahead without incident!

CHAPTER 9

The Audit Process

REMEMBER WHY YOU ARE THERE

Before we launch into the mechanics of the audit process, it is prudent to recall why you are performing the audit. It is to obtain objective evidence and so determine if the audit objectives are satisfied. Primarily, is the system implemented, is it effective, are there areas for improvement, and as a result can the audit team give a positive recommendation about the organization?

Objective evidence is sought through interviews, asking, What? When? Where? Who? Why? and How? and of course the most important element, Show me. This latter request is not a matter of disbelief, but it is the auditor's role to make a decision based on objective evidence rather than anecdotal testament.

Objective evidence may also be sought through:

- examination of documents;
- examination of records;
- verification of products; and
- verification of equipment.

It is not an acceptable protocol to involve suppliers or customers of the organization in an ISO 9001:2000-based audit.

QUESTIONING STYLE

A certain "God complex" has crept into the persona of many an auditor. Because the auditor is rarely challenged and perceived as the undeniable expert, this trait is understandable, however flawed it might be. But the God complex contributes to "arrogance" in the auditor's posture, which is cold and intimidating and does little to facilitate the audit process.

Skilled auditors have the capacity to put people at ease. They engage in "small talk" just long enough to allow the auditee to settle in, and then progress through the necessary questions at a pace that is commensurate with the auditee's comfort and the time management required of the overall program.

Auditors do not learn things by asking questions but by listening to the answers. That is a fine point but an important one. The auditee must be allowed to speak freely, without a sense of intimidation or fear.

Because the quality assurance psyche is one of prevention, it is good audit practice to ask hypothetical questions: "What would you do if . . . ?" This tests the robustness of the procedure or process document.

When dealing with managers, recognize that one is dealing with potential politicians and thus the answer one gets may not relate directly to the question that has been asked. Be persistent; repeat or rephrase questions. Do not be sidetracked or bullied away from a topic.

The most underutilized of all questioning styles is the "silent question." This is where the auditor leaves a pause. Auditees do not like pauses. They like to fill pauses, and often they volunteer items (despite their managers having told them not to!). Such items are very often worth pursuing.

Ensure that the wording of the question is suitable for the person being interviewed; avoid the jargon of the standard. Spend an appropriate amount of time with managerial and operational personnel. Asking the same question at different levels in the hierarchy can give interesting results.

Remember that the question as worded on the checklist is probably not how you will ask it of any auditee, and certainly not of every auditee. Questions pertaining to policy, results, and tasks need to be adapted to the issue, the circumstances, and the type of auditee.

When working in noisy areas, give consideration to the auditee and to yourself so that both parties can be heard. Never be tempted to remove ear protection in an area where it is mandated.

Finally, if things are good, say so. Being complimentary is not against the rules, and it actually helps if eventually you do find a nonconformity. It gives balance to the process.

PERSONAL DEMEANOR

The lifestyle of an auditor appears, at first, glamorous. Jet-setting here, there, and everywhere. But auditors spend hundreds of nights a year alone in hotels and ask the same sort of questions, of the same sort of people, getting the same sort of answers, year after year after year. It is unsurprising then that at four P.M. on the fourth day of the four hundred forty-fourth audit the mind of the auditor begins to wander and a misty look comes upon his or her countenance. Maintaining enthusiasm, energy, and interest can be difficult. So a good diet, a regular sleep pattern, and breaks every hour or so, just to stop and think, are essential. Looking interested, using positive body language such as nodding one's head, and repeating a little of what the auditee has just said to you all send out the right signals.

It is good practice as well as good manners to be polite, courteous, and helpful to an auditee. One should not revel in an auditee's anxiety or nervous disposition. The most skilled of operators will often break something when the auditor is standing behind them. Go easy; be gentle with them!

The auditor's eyes and face are, of course, his or her worst enemy because they often belie the true sense of the auditor's reaction to the answer the auditee has just given. Not appearing to be distrusting is very important. Take care with that raised eyebrow or that tongue in cheek. It can backfire, with serious repercussions.

There are also some auditees who enjoy an auditor's discomfort or apparent lack of expertise. They may ask the auditor to climb a ladder to the top of a refinery to check a meter when there is a closed-circuit television camera that could have zoomed in on the device from the warmth and relative safety of the control office (yes, this happened). When such things happen, remaining calm and seeing the funny side is a virtue. Least said, soonest mended!

At the end of the interview, the auditee's office is likely to look untidy. Some of them are like that when one enters, but the reason for the lack of order on the auditor's departure is that several files have been examined, records checked, procedures read, and products explained, and all these things are now strewn around the auditee's desk. Offer to help the auditee to put things back, and watch the reaction! They cannot wait to get rid of you, so none of them ever accepts the offer (but it is fun to watch that reaction).

ELEPHANTS HAVE GOOD MEMORIES; AUDITORS MAKE NOTES

Making notes is an important part of the auditor's process. Recording such details as dates, names, products, locations, batch numbers and so on is vital if a complete report is to be presented to the auditee's management team. If, at the closing meeting, the auditor states that a design plan showed no evidence of being updated, the management team is perfectly right to ask, "Which one?" It would be good to have recorded the number. As a tip, it is suggested that any document that one intends to use as a reference should be referred to the escort and copies made if possible. At the very least, establish how the organization would locate the document if it were to look for it again. Would it be by customer name, project number, date, or other? It is no good for the auditor to record the customer name if the organization indexes the record by project number.

Making notes is a discipline. It is something that for the first 30 minutes of an audit, all auditors are good at. As the audit progresses and becomes interesting, perhaps even educational, the notes become more and more abbreviated. They are written on pieces of paper, the back of the checklist, or the palm of the hand, and six hours later as the auditor compiles the report he or she finds the notes are somewhat disjointed.

Make notes about everything that happens. Be prepared to stop the interview and explain that you are taking notes. Do not make notes only of the things that are wrong. Auditees get wise to this very quickly and learn when to interject with new evidence or lunch!

Never leave checklists or notes in an accessible place when going to lunch. In some organizations, when the auditor returns, everyone seems to know the questions that are being asked. Curious, that?!

Making notes takes time. They must be logical and structured, as well as legible. Balancing the clipboard on one knee, with the standard, quality manual, and procedures under one arm and checklists and copies of documentation in the other does not lend itself to the neatest of handwriting.

OBJECTIVE EVIDENCE

Good auditors follow one rule: No objective evidence = no finding. Objective evidence is the proof that something complies or does not; that something is effective or is not. Objective evidence can be in the following forms:

- Documents (date, title, serial number, revision level)
- Equipment (description, serial number, date of calibration or maintenance, location)
- Records (product, results, dates, names of people)
- People (job title, name, department)
- Products (description, part number, location, status, batch number)
- Locations (department name, zone reference, bay number)

Relying on a verbal agreement can be dangerous. It is open to misinterpretation; sometimes auditees claim that they did not say something (this is a rare event).

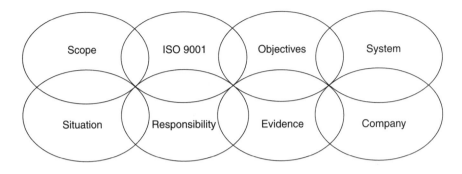

Figure 9.1 Factors to be taken into account when recording a finding.

When recording a finding, the auditor needs to consider several criteria (see Figure 9.1). The scope and objectives will help determine the relevance of the finding. The standard and the company's system will determine if the finding is worthy of further investigation or perhaps if it is a potential nonconformity. The situation in which the finding is made will determine whether the circumstances are appropriate (for example, overhearing two managers arguing about the way in which equipment is selected does not justify a nonconformity). That the person with whom one is speaking has responsibility for the item being discussed merits verification before recording what is said.

A note here about the use of video cameras, cassette recorders, and photographic cameras: The former two are taboo and should not be used, especially to record what an auditee is saying. It is a sure way of getting him or her to say nothing. The photographic camera can be useful to capture incidents (for example, leaking equipment). It is vital that auditors get permission before taking photographs. It might be something worth considering at the opening meeting.

To ensure that the finding is understandable to all concerned, capture all the pertinent details about it so as to have adequate objective evidence to present to the management team, and then place the finding in the context of the type of company where the audit is being performed.

AUDITOR TACTICS

Presenting the correct image is another attribute professional auditors must strive for. This extends from the way the auditor dresses to the auditor's expression of experience and confidence to the words he or she uses and the style he or she adopts.

Correct behaviors include avoiding commenting on previous audits, especially those in other organizations, and not making sexist, racist, or other inappropriate comments. In addition, as mentioned earlier, it is important to give a sense of balance when presenting the findings. The auditor may be seen as firm but must also seem fair, realistic, and pragmatic.

One of the core competencies within the category of behavior is courage. This may sound strange, but it takes immense courage to stand in front of a board of directors of an international company and make a negative recommendation. Too many auditors lack this capacity for conviction, and this weakness in character leads to more organizations receiving a positive recommendation than should be the case. If the auditor cannot master this final and most uncomfortable of scenarios, he or she should not begin the process.

The courage factor is also relevant when nonconformities are detected; the auditor must raise these immediately with the escort and/or the local manager. Being brave is so much easier when one is certain of one's facts. If there is objective evidence to support a nonconformity, then there *is* a nonconformity and getting the agreement of the auditee is less difficult. Still, saying the words "This is a nonconformity—do you agree?" takes courage. Other auditors are a little too gleeful when they get to utter those words, out of some perverse sense of pleasure taken in identifying nonconformities. This "satisfaction" factor is equally inappropriate.

A third-party auditor avoids being drawn into giving advice. Such is not his or her role, and making suggestions or recommendations can cause avoidable complications. In a second-party situation, it will depend on the relationship. But internally, during first-party audits, discussions about possible solutions are common. The rule is that irrespective of the type of audit, the responsibility for corrective action lies with the auditee.

AUDITEE TACTICS

The nightmare celebrities that appear in role-play scenarios in auditor training courses are, fortunately, rare in real life. They do exist, though, and dealing with them is an important skill for auditors.

They fall into several categories:

- Time wasters (arrive late for interviews, have to keep going out of the office to look for files, are continually interrupted)
- Those who provoke (challenge the age, the competence, or the integrity of the auditor)

- Those who always have an excuse (special cases)
- Those who might try to bribe the auditor (very rare, but be careful of golf umbrellas, crystal, and extravagant meals)
- Those who glorify the auditor (give false praise and build an imaginary friendship)
- The vital workers and the absent (Ask what happens in the event of the vital worker being away from work for an extended period. Be cautious of the sick, lame, and lazy who suddenly cannot move quickly, lift boxes, or climb stairs.)

THINGS THAT CAN GO WRONG

In our discussion of the opening meeting, where things normally go well, we included a long list of what could go wrong. During the execution of the audit, things often go wrong as well. The list is too long to give it in its entirety, but here are some of the more common problems for you to ponder:

- The auditee goes missing
- The auditee gets violent
- Two auditees get into an argument
- The auditee claims that what you have discovered is actually better than the specification
- The auditee claims that the auditor has acted inappropriately
- The auditee makes short-term corrections to the issues without addressing the root cause of the problem
- The reality of how people are working is nothing like what is specified in the procedure or process documents
- The auditee explains that the reason for not complying with a requirement is that there are insufficient resources

A few minutes considering your response in each of these situations in the calmness of reading this book will enable you to respond professionally should one of them happen in reality.

CHAPTER 10

Reporting Findings and Nonconformities

HOW AND WHEN TO REPORT AUDIT FINDINGS

Audit findings are brought to the attention of the escorts and local managers throughout the audit process—this avoids surprises at the closing meeting. During longer audits, the audit team may make interim presentations to the management team.

The first formal presentation of the total audit findings is at the closing meeting. This is the task of the lead auditor and other team members, each, usually, presenting his or her own findings. A written report will follow either immediately after the closing meeting or within a short period of time.

The method of audit reporting should cover each of the following topics:

- Scope
- Objectives
- Strengths
- Nonconformities
- Areas for improvement
- Conclusions
- Recommendations

The preceding headings are in addition to the following obvious information:

- Name of company
- Personnel interviewed
- Dates
- Program
- Standard or other document references
- Auditee

After the auditee has addressed the issues highlighted in the report, he or she should be able to observe that their business has improved.

Value-adding reporting ensures that there is a positive response from the organization. This means that the report must be seen as fair. Avoiding trivia and highlighting not only the problems but also the strengths is an important demonstration of balance. It is not wise for the report to be consultative—that is, proposing approaches for the organization to follow to address a nonconformity. The role of the report is to ensure that the objectives are addressed, and the conclusions of the report should address them specifically.

The tone of the report should be encouraging rather than critical, reducing the risk of adversarial responses but ensuring a positive acceptance of the issues raised and a willingness to implement corrective action.

CLASSIFICATION OF NONCONFORMITIES

Before committing the audit team to declaring a nonconformity, the lead auditor should consider the following questions:

- Is this an isolated incident?
- Is this happening frequently?
- Are these findings consistent with the scope and objectives?
- Is there tangible objective evidence?
- Do we have agreement?
- Is this a major system breakdown or a minor lapse?

A nonconformity is an instance where some specified requirement has not been satisfied. This could be a requirement of the standard, contract, system, or quality plan.

Nonconformities may be categorized thusly:

Category	Interpretation
Major	The company does not meet the requirements of:
	• the standard.
	• the contract.
	The company does not do what it claims.
	There is a significant gap in the system.
Minor	Occasional, insignificant lapses are noted.
	The company is doing more than required. (Will it always happen?)
	The nonconformity has no impact on the product.

This rather simplistic approach suggests that if something is a mandatory requirement and the organization does not meet it, then that constitutes a major nonconformity. So, for example, if one record cannot be found, that would be a major nonconformity. In some industries (for example, the nuclear industry) this may be justified, but in most circumstances such a classification would seem harsh.

A minor nonconformity is recorded when a value-adding activity is discovered that is not in the process documents or procedures. Failure to do this may result in the new practice never being incorporated in the documents, and when new people join the company, they will revert to the prescribed method, thus losing the improved method.

The consequences of classifying the nonconformities are as follows:

- Major—would prevent recommendation of certification
- Minor—would not normally prevent recommendation of certification
- Observation/Comments—would not prevent recommendation of certification

This being the case a more robust approach is required to classify any nonconformity. A flowchart (see Figure 10.1) is proposed as the basis for this most sensitive of audit decisions.

In Figure 10.1 the primary concern is *impact on the product*. The purpose of any system is to ensure that products or services conform with specified requirements. If a nonconformity directly compromises this, it is a major problem. Mandatory requirements of either the standard or the organization's own system (that is, where the term *shall* is used) normally require more than one example to classify the nonconformity as major. Nonconformities that affect everyone or everything are major. If none of these conditions is answered with a "yes" the nonconformity is probably minor, if there is a nonconformity at all.

All parties must understand the process for raising a nonconformity. That process is shown in Figure 10.2. To raise a nonconformity the lead auditor and audit team members should ensure that the following criteria are met:

- Clear definition of the problem
- Clear and unambiguous objective evidence
- Capacity to explain the nonconformity and the consequences thereof for the business and in the context of the audit process
- Contingency plan that addresses potential questions or challenges
- Clear support information (for example, location, name of auditee and/or escort, reference documents, records, products, equipment and/or materials)
- Clear indication of which clause in the standard, contract, and/or system documents has been violated

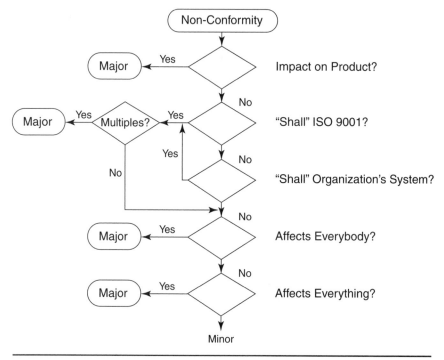

Figure 10.1 Classifying a nonconformity.
Source: Eurospan Developments Ltd. QMS Auditor/Lead Auditor Course 2000, section 14. Used with permission.

The typical mistakes made on nonconformity reports are listed below:

- Putting multiple nonconformities relating to different clauses of the standard on the same nonconformity report
- Replicates of the same type of problem being recorded on different nonconformity reports, instead of raising one report with multiple pieces of evidence

Raising a nonconformity that addresses a trivial issue will merit more debate about the classification of the nonconformity and the integrity of the process than it is worth; nit-picking is to be avoided.

To avoid potential misunderstandings, the auditor should write nonconformities as problems and not solutions (for example, "There is no quality policy," not "The company should implement a quality policy").

All nonconformities must be agreed to and signed either at the time they are found or at the closing meeting. The latter is the preferred option as teams of auditors may have found similar problems, and only when they review the findings together can they classify them.

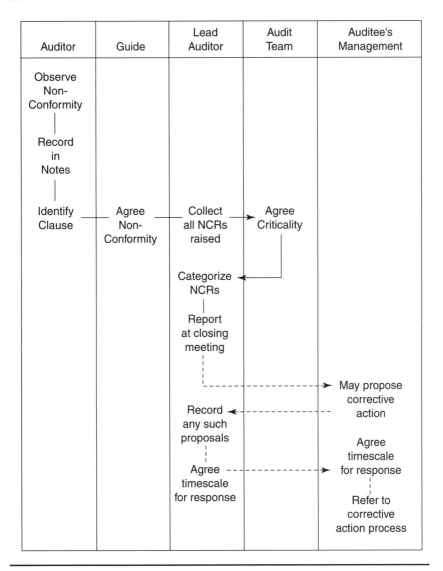

Figure 10.2 The process for raising a nonconformity.

Source: Eurospan Developments Ltd. QMS Auditor/Lead Auditor Course 2000, section 14. Used with permission.

The nonconformity reports are to be treated confidentially and should be retained for a defined period. Subsequent audit teams should have access to these records to develop a history of the auditee's performance.

A sample audit report is shown in Figure 10.3 and sample nonconformity reports are shown in Figures 10.4 and 10.5.

AUDIT REPORT		No.: 0127	
COMPANY	XYZ plc	DATE	02/01/2001

KEY PERSONNEL	AUDIT TEAM
J. Smyth—Chief Executive A. Button—Manufacturing Director M. Reece—Quality Manager A. Crabbe—Design Manager J. Rushmore—Production Manager	Brighton Projects Inc. P. Perfect—Lead Auditor J. Bull S. Brown
AUDIT STANDARD	ISO 9001:2000

REPORT *1 of 2*

OVERVIEW

Scope: Design, development, and manufacture of special purpose pneumatic drive systems.

Objectives: To determine, for the purpose of certification, the extent of conformity of the system with ISO 9001:2000 and its effectiveness in ensuring that products meet specified requirements.

Audit Findings:

Date of audit: 02 01 2001
Location: Chipping Down, Hants

The company's quality manual was examined in advance of the on-site audit and was found to address fully the application of ISO 9001 within XYZ plc.

Procedures in the manufacturing function are well established and appear to be working effectively across all current product lines. Manufacture is initiated through the planning group where a closed loop system is operated from customer requirements to final release of product.

Internal audit is an established function, and reports indicate a positive approach to quality management and customer satisfaction. The schedule should be extended to cover new areas as further procedures are implemented.

During the on-site audit it became apparent that in a number of key areas the system has yet to be fully implemented.

In particular:

    Customer-related processes
    Design control—planning, verification, and validation
    Purchasing—selection of subcontractors
    Corrective and preventive Action
    Training

Figure 10.3 A sample audit report.

AUDIT REPORT	No.: 0127

NCRs RAISED

Number of NCRs raised : 2

Major
NCR Number 1—Competency identification

Minor
NCR Number 2—Document control

CONCLUSIONS

Whilst the company has done much to implement an effective quality system, it does not at this time satisfy the requirements of ISO 9001.

The preparation and implementation of operating procedures and process documentation in the sales and design functions have not been fully deployed and do not ensure that products meet specified requirements.

Whilst the control of manufacture would appear to be sound, a number of opportunities for improvement exist.

RECOMMENDATIONS

Based on the findings of the audit and subsequent conclusions, it is not possible at this time to recommend this organization for certification.

At the closing meeting, it was agreed that a follow-up visit will be conducted in 13 weeks after corrective action has been taken on the two nonconformities raised.

Signed: P. Perfect	Name: P. Perfect—Lead Auditor	Date: 02/01/2001

Figure 10.3   Continued.

NONCONFORMITY REPORT			No.: 0127/1	

COMPANY	XYZ plc			
DEPARTMENT	Design and Development		DATE	02/01/2001
AUDIT STANDARD		ISO 9001:2000		

State the finding including the objective evidence:

Process controls do not include the identification of skills and the training needs for project design staff. As a result three contracts have been lost due to the new product introduction time quoted by XYZ plc.

Process procedure DC 016A—Design and Development planning is in draft, but this does not address the skills requirement.

ISO 9001 Requirement	6.2.2 (a)	MAJOR / ~~MINOR~~	delete N/A

State the nonconformity:

The organization has not identified the necessary competence for project design staff.

AUDITOR	S. Brown	COMPANY REPRESENTATIVE	A. Crabbe

CORRECTIVE ACTION

TARGET DATE		SIGNED:	

FOLLOW-UP FINDINGS

DATE:		SIGNED:	

Figure 10.4 Nonconformity report (major).

NONCONFORMITY REPORT		No.: 0127/2

COMPANY	XYZ plc		
DEPARTMENT	No. 3 Assembly Area	DATE	02/01/2001

AUDIT STANDARD	ISO 9001:2000

State the finding including the objective evidence:

Document control—Workshop Drawings

Two of the workshop drawings examined were found to be at the wrong issue level.

Valve drive mechanism 02-0875-027 Issue G should be Issue K.

Pump case 11-1275-001 Issue B should be Issue C.

The amount of scrap caused by these two errors has been £14,000.

ISO 9001 Requirement | 4.2.3 (g) | | MAJOR / MINOR delete N/A |

State the nonconformity:

Procedures for the control of documents have not prevented the unintended use of obsolete documents.

AUDITOR	J. Bull	COMPANY REPRESENTATIVE	J. Rushmore

CORRECTIVE ACTION

TARGET DATE		SIGNED:	

FOLLOW-UP FINDINGS

DATE:		SIGNED:	

Figure 10.5   Nonconformity report (minor).

Auditors need to ensure that the conclusions relate to the audit objectives—that is, if the objective is to determine the extent of conformity and effectiveness of the system, then the conclusions should reflect those two criteria.

Recommendations normally fall into three categories:

- Recommend approval
- Recommend nonapproval
- Recommend approval but with stated conditions

WORDING OF POTENTIAL NONCONFORMITIES

When putting a nonconformity into words it is important to stay close to the wording of the standard. The following sections consist of examples of such wording presented under the respective clause of ISO 9001:2000.

4.1 General requirements*

The organization has not established, documented, implemented, and/or maintained a quality management system.

The organization has not continually improved its effectiveness in accordance with the requirements of this international standard.

The organization has not:

- (a) identified the processes needed for the quality management system and/or their application throughout the organization;
- (b) determined the sequence and interaction of the processes;
- (c) determined criteria and methods needed to ensure that both the operation and control of the processes are effective;
- (d) ensured the availability of resources and information necessary to support the operation and monitoring of the processes;
- (e) monitored, measured, and analyzed the processes; and
- (f) implemented actions necessary to achieve planned results and continual improvement of the processes.

The processes are not managed by the organization in accordance with the requirements of the international standard.

Where the organization has chosen to outsource any process that affects product conformity with requirements, the organization has not ensured control over such processes.

Control of outsourced processes has not been identified in the quality management system.

*Note: Where a requirement states, for example, "established, documented, implemented," the organization may not have done any of these things or may have done only one or two. The wording of the nonconformity must reflect exactly what was found.

4.2 Documentation requirements

4.2.1 General

The quality management system documentation does not include:

    (a) documented statements of a quality policy and quality objectives;
    (b) a quality manual;
    (c) documented procedures required by the international standard;
    (d) documents needed by the organization to ensure the effective planning, operation, and control of its processes; and
    (e) records required by the international standard.

4.2.2 Quality manual

The organization has not established and/or maintained a quality manual that includes:

    (a) the scope of the quality management system, including details of and justification for any exclusions;
    (b) the documented procedures established for the quality management system, or reference to them; and
    (c) a description of the interaction between the processes of the quality management system.

4.2.3 Control of documents

Documents required by the quality management system are not controlled.

    Records are a special type of document and have not been controlled according to the requirements given in clause 4.2.4 of ISO 9001:2000.

    A documented procedure has not been established to define the controls needed to:

    (a) approve documents for adequacy prior to issue;
    (b) review and update as necessary and reapprove documents;
    (c) ensure that changes and the current revision status of documents are identified;
    (d) ensure that relevant versions of applicable documents are available at points of use;
    (e) ensure that documents remain legible and readily identifiable;
    (f) ensure that documents of external origin are identified and their distribution controlled; and
    (g) prevent the unintended use of obsolete documents and to apply suitable identification to them if they are retained for any purpose.

4.2.4 Control of records

Records have not been established and maintained to provide evidence of conformity to requirements and of the effective operation of the quality management system.

Records are not legible, readily identifiable, and/or retrievable.

A documented procedure has not been established to define the controls needed for the identification, storage, protection, retrieval, retention time, and/or disposition of records.

5 Management responsibility

5.1 Management commitment

Top management has not provided evidence of its commitment to the development and implementation of the quality management system and/or continually improving its effectiveness by:

(a) communicating to the organization the importance of meeting customer as well as statutory and regulatory requirements;
(b) establishing the quality policy;
(c) ensuring that quality objectives are established;
(d) conducting management reviews; and
(e) ensuring the availability of resources.

5.2 Customer focus

Top management has not ensured that customer requirements are determined and are met with the aim of enhancing customer satisfaction.

5.3 Quality policy

Top management has not ensured that the quality policy:

(a) is appropriate to the purpose of the organization;
(b) includes a commitment to comply with requirements and continually improve the effectiveness of the quality management system;
(c) provides a framework for establishing and reviewing quality objectives;
(d) is communicated and understood within the organization; and
(e) is reviewed for continuing suitability.

5.4 Planning

5.4.1 Quality objectives

Top management has not ensured that quality objectives, including those needed to meet requirements for product, have been established at relevant functions and levels within the organization.

The quality objectives are not measurable and/or consistent with the quality policy.

5.4.2 Quality management system planning

Top management has not ensured that:

(a) the planning of the quality management system is carried out in order to meet the requirements given in clause 4.1 of ISO 901:2000 and/or the quality objectives; and

(b) the integrity of the quality management system is maintained when changes to the quality management system are planned and implemented.

5.5 Responsibility, authority, and communication

5.5.1 Responsibility and authority

Top management has not ensured that responsibilities and authorities are defined and communicated within the organization.

5.5.2 Management representative

Top management has not appointed a member of management who, irrespective of other responsibilities, has responsibility and authority that includes:

(a) ensuring that processes needed for the quality management system are established, implemented, and maintained;

(b) reporting to top management on the performance of the quality management system and any need for improvement; and

(c) ensuring the promotion of awareness of customer requirements throughout the organization.

5.5.3 Internal communication

Top management has not ensured that appropriate communication processes are established within the organization and/or that communication takes place regarding the effectiveness of the quality management system.

5.6 Management review

5.6.1 General

Top management has not reviewed the organization's quality management system at planned intervals to ensure its continuing suitability, adequacy, and effectiveness.

The review does not include assessing opportunities for improvement and/or the need for changes to the quality management system, including the quality policy and quality objectives.

Records from management reviews have not been maintained.

5.6.2 Review input

The input to management review does not include information on:

    (a) results of audits;
    (b) customer feedback;
    (c) process performance and product conformity;
    (d) status of preventive and corrective actions;
    (e) follow-up actions from previous management reviews;
    (f) changes that could affect the quality management system; and
    (g) recommendations for improvement.

5.6.3 Review output

The output from the management review does not include any decisions and actions related to:

    (a) improvement of the effectiveness of the quality management system and its processes;
    (b) improvement of product related to customer requirements; and
    (c) resource needs.

6 Resource management

6.1 Provision of resources

The organization has not determined and/or provided the resources needed to:

    (a) implement and maintain the quality management system and continually improve its effectiveness; and
    (b) enhance customer satisfaction by meeting customer requirements.

6.2 Human resources

6.2.1 General

The organization cannot demonstrate that personnel performing work affecting product quality are competent on the basis of appropriate education, training, skills, and experience.

6.2.2 Competence, awareness, and training

The organization has not:

(a) determined the necessary competence for personnel performing work affecting product quality;

(b) provided training or taken other actions to satisfy these needs;

(c) evaluated the effectiveness of the actions taken;

(d) ensured that its personnel are aware of the relevance and importance of their activities and how they contribute to the achievement of the quality objectives; and

(e) maintained appropriate records of education, training, skills, and experience.

6.3 Infrastructure

The organization has not determined, provided, and/or maintained the infrastructure needed to achieve conformity to product requirements.

6.4 Work environment

The organization has not determined and managed the work environment needed to achieve conformity to product requirements.

7 Product realization

7.1 Planning of product realization

The organization has not planned and developed the processes needed for product realization.

Planning of product realization is not consistent with the requirements of the other processes of the quality management system.

In planning product realization, the organization has not determined, as appropriate:

(a) quality objectives and requirements for the product;

(b) the need to establish processes and documents and provide resources specific to the product;

(c) required verification, validation, monitoring, inspection, and test activities specific to the product and the criteria for product acceptance; and

(d) records needed to provide evidence that the realization processes and resulting product meet requirements.

Output of the planning of product realization is not in a form suitable for the organization's method of operations.

7.2 Customer-related processes

7.2.1 Determination of requirements related to the product

The organization has not determined:

(a) requirements specified by the customer, including the requirements for delivery and postdelivery activities;

(b) requirements not stated by the customer but necessary for specified or intended use, where known;

(c) statutory and regulatory requirements related to the product; and

(d) any additional requirements determined by the organization.

7.2.2 Review of requirements related to the product

The organization has not reviewed the requirements related to the product.

Review of product requirements has not been conducted prior to the organization's commitment to supply a product to the customer.

The organization has not ensured that:

(a) product requirements are defined;

(b) contract or order requirements differing from those previously expressed are resolved; and

(c) the organization has the ability to meet the defined requirements.

Records of the results of the review and actions arising from the review have not been maintained.

Where the customer provides no documented statement of requirement, the customer requirements have not been confirmed by the organization before acceptance.

Where product requirements are changed, the organization has not ensured that relevant documents are amended and/or that relevant personnel are made aware of the changed requirements.

7.2.3 Customer communication

The organization has not determined and/or implemented effective arrangements for communicating with customers in relation to:

(a) product information;
(b) inquiries, contracts, or order handling, including amendments; and
(c) customer feedback, including customer complaints.

7.3 Design and development

7.3.1 Design and development planning

The organization has not planned and/or controlled the design and development of product.

During the design and development planning, the organization has not determined:

(a) the design and development stages;
(b) the review, verification, and validation that are appropriate to each design and development stage; and
(c) the responsibilities and authorities for design and development.

The organization has not managed the interfaces between different groups involved in design and development to ensure effective communication and/or clear assignment of responsibility.

Planning output has not been updated, as appropriate, as the design and development progresses.

7.3.2 Design and development inputs

Inputs relating to product requirements have not been determined and/or records have not been maintained.

Design and development inputs do not include:

(a) functional and performance requirements;
(b) applicable statutory and regulatory requirements;
(c) where applicable, information derived from previous similar designs; and
(d) other requirements essential for design and development.

Design and development inputs are not reviewed for adequacy.

Design and development requirements are not complete and unambiguous and/or are in conflict with each other.

7.3.3 Design and development outputs

The outputs of design and development are not provided in a form that enables verification against the design and/or development input and are not approved prior to release.

Design and development outputs do not:

(a) meet the input requirements for design and development;
(b) provide appropriate information for purchasing, production, and for service provision;
(c) contain or reference product acceptance criteria; and
(d) specify the characteristics of the product that are essential for its safe and proper use.

7.3.4 Design and development review

At suitable stages, systematic reviews of design and development are not performed in accordance with planned arrangements to:

(a) evaluate the ability of the results of design and development to meet requirements; and
(b) identify any problems and propose necessary actions.

Participants in design and development reviews do not include representatives of functions concerned with the design and development stage(s) being reviewed.

Records of the results of the design and development reviews and/or any necessary actions are not maintained.

7.3.5 Design and development verification

Verification is not performed in accordance with planned arrangements to ensure that the design and development outputs have met the design and development input requirements.

Records of the results of the verification and any necessary actions are not maintained.

7.3.6 Design and development validation

Design and development validation is not performed in accordance with planned arrangements to ensure that the resulting product is capable of meeting the requirements for the specified application or intended use, where known.

Wherever practicable, validation is not completed prior to the delivery or implementation of the product.

Records of the results of validation and any necessary actions are not maintained (see clause 4.2.4).

7.3.7 Control of design and development changes

Design and development changes are not identified and/or records are not maintained.

Design changes are not reviewed, verified, and/or validated, as appropriate, and/or approved before implementation.

The review of design and development changes does not include evaluation of the effect of the changes on constituent parts and product already delivered.

Records of the results of the review of changes and any necessary actions are not maintained.

7.4 Purchasing

7.4.1 Purchasing process

The organization has not ensured that purchased product conforms to specified purchase requirements.

The type and extent of control applied to the supplier and the purchased product is not dependent upon the effect of the purchased product on subsequent product realization or the final product.

The organization has not evaluated and/or selected suppliers based on their ability to supply product in accordance with the organization's requirements.

Criteria for selection, evaluation, and reevaluation are not established.

Records of the results of evaluations and any necessary actions arising from the evaluation are not maintained.

7.4.2 Purchasing information

Purchasing information does not describe the product to be purchased, including where appropriate:

(a) requirements for approval of product, procedures, processes, and equipment;
(b) requirements for qualification of personnel; and
(c) quality management system requirements.

The organization does not ensure the adequacy of specified purchase requirements prior to their communication to the supplier.

7.4.3 Verification of purchased product

The organization does not establish and implement the inspection or other activities necessary for ensuring that purchased product meets specified purchase requirements.

Where the organization or its customer intends to perform verification at the supplier's premises, the organization has not stated the intended verification arrangements and/or method of product release in the purchasing information.

7.5 Production and service provision

7.5.1 Control of production and service provision

The organization does not plan and carry out production and service provision under controlled conditions.

Controlled conditions do not include, as applicable:

(a) the availability of information that describes the characteristics of the product;
(b) the availability of work instructions, as necessary;
(c) the use of suitable equipment;
(d) the availability and use of monitoring and measuring devices;
(e) the implementation of monitoring and measurement; and
(f) the implementation of release, delivery, and postdelivery activities.

7.5.2 Validation of processes for production and service provision

The organization does not validate any processes for production and service provision where the resulting output cannot be verified by subsequent monitoring or measurement.

Validation of processes does not demonstrate the ability of such processes to achieve planned results.

The organization does not establish arrangements for such processes, including as applicable:

(a) defined criteria for review and approval of the processes;
(b) approval of equipment and qualification of personnel;
(c) use of specific methods and procedures;
(d) requirements for records; and
(e) revalidation.

7.5.3 Identification and traceability

Where appropriate, the organization does not identify the product by suitable means throughout product realization.

The organization does not identify the product status with respect to monitoring and measurement requirements.

Where traceability is a requirement, the organization does not control and record the unique identification of the product.

7.5.4 Customer property

The organization does not exercise care with customer property while it is under the organization's control or being used by the organization.

The organization does not identify, verify, protect, and/or safeguard customer property provided for use or incorporation into the product.

Where customer property is lost, damaged, or otherwise found to be unsuitable for use, this is not reported to the customer and/or records are not maintained.

7.5.5 Preservation of product

The organization has not preserved the conformity of product during internal processing and delivery to the intended destination. This preservation does not include identification, handling, packaging, storage, and protection. Preservation has not been applied to the constituent parts of a product.

7.6 Control of monitoring and measuring devices

The organization does not determine the monitoring and measurement to be undertaken and the monitoring and/or measuring devices needed to provide evidence of conformity of product to determined requirements.

The organization does not establish processes to ensure that monitoring and measurement can be carried out and/or are carried out in a manner that is consistent with the monitoring and measurement requirements.

Where necessary to ensure valid results, measuring equipment:

(a) is not calibrated or verified at specified intervals, or prior to use, against measurement standards traceable to international or national measurement standards. Where no such standards exist, the basis used for calibration or verification is not recorded;
(b) adjusted or readjusted as necessary;
(c) identified to enable the calibration status to be determined;
(d) safeguarded from adjustments that would invalidate the measurement result; and
(e) protected from damage and deterioration during handling, maintenance, and storage.

The organization does not assess and/or record the validity of the previous measuring results when the equipment is found not to conform to requirements.

The organization does not take appropriate action on the equipment and any product affected when the equipment is found not to conform to requirements.

Records of the results of calibration and verification are not maintained.

When computer software is used in the monitoring and measurement of specified requirements, the ability of the software to satisfy the intended application is not confirmed.

The ability of computer software to satisfy the intended application is not confirmed prior to initial use and reconfirmed as necessary.

8 Measurement, analysis, and improvement

8.1 General

The organization does not plan and implement the monitoring, measurement, analysis, and improvement processes needed:

(a) to demonstrate conformity of the product;
(b) to ensure conformity of the quality management system; and
(c) to continually improve the effectiveness of the quality management system.

Monitoring, measurement, analysis, and improvement processes do not include determination of applicable methods, including statistical techniques, and the extent of their use.

8.2 Monitoring and measurement

8.2.1 Customer satisfaction

As one of the measurements of the performance of the quality management system, the organization does not monitor information relating to customer perception as to whether the organization has met customer requirements.

The methods for obtaining and using information relating to customer perception as to whether the organization has met customer requirements are not determined.

8.2.2 Internal audit

The organization does not conduct internal audits at planned intervals to determine whether the quality management system:

(a) conforms to the planned arrangements and/or to the requirements of ISO 9001:2000 and/or to the quality management system requirements established by the organization;
(b) is effectively implemented and maintained.

An audit program is not planned taking into consideration the status and importance of the processes and areas to be audited, as well as the results of previous audits.

The audit criteria, scope, frequency, and/or methods are not defined.

Selection of auditors and conduct of audits does not ensure objectivity and impartiality of the audit process.

Auditors audit their own work.

The responsibilities and requirements for planning and conducting audits, and for reporting results and/or maintaining records, are not defined in a documented procedure.

The management responsible for the area being audited does not ensure that actions are taken without undue delay to eliminate detected nonconformities and their causes.

Follow-up activities do not include the verification of the actions taken and the reporting of verification results.

8.2.3 Monitoring and measurement of processes

The organization does not apply suitable methods for monitoring and, where applicable, measurement of the quality management system processes.

The methods for monitoring and, where applicable, measurement of the quality management system processes do not demonstrate the ability of the processes to achieve planned results.

When planned results are not achieved, correction and corrective action is not taken, as appropriate, to ensure conformity of the product.

8.2.4 Monitoring and measurement of product

The organization does not monitor and measure the characteristics of the product to verify that product requirements have been met.

Monitoring and measuring the characteristics of the product to verify that product requirements have been met is not carried out at appropriate stages of the product realization process in accordance with the planned arrangements.

Evidence of conformity with the acceptance criteria is not maintained.

Records do not indicate the person(s) authorizing release of product.

Product release or service delivery proceeds before the planned arrangements have been satisfactorily completed. There is no evidence of approval by a relevant authority and, where applicable, by the customer.

8.3 Control of nonconforming product

The organization does not ensure that product that does not conform to product requirements is identified and controlled to prevent its unintended use or delivery.

The controls and related responsibilities and authorities for dealing with nonconforming product are not defined in a documented procedure.

The organization does not deal with nonconforming product in one or more of the following ways:

(a) By taking action to eliminate the detected nonconformity
(b) By authorizing its use, release, or acceptance under concession by a relevant authority and, where applicable, by the customer
(c) By taking action to preclude its original intended use or application

Records of the nature of nonconformities and any subsequent actions taken, including concessions obtained, are not maintained.

When nonconforming product is corrected it is not subject to reverification to demonstrate conformity to the requirements.

When nonconforming product is detected after delivery or use has started, the organization does not take action appropriate to the effects, or potential effects, of the nonconformity.

8.4 Analysis of data

The organization does not determine, collect, and/or analyze appropriate data to demonstrate the suitability and effectiveness of the quality management system and to evaluate where continual improvement of the effectiveness of the quality management system can be made.

Data to demonstrate the suitability and effectiveness of the quality management system and to evaluate where continual improvement of the effectiveness of the quality management system can be made does not include data generated as a result of monitoring and measurement and from other relevant sources.

The analysis of data does not provide information relating to:

(a) customer satisfaction;
(b) conformity to product requirements;
(c) characteristics and trends of processes and products including opportunities for preventive action; and
(d) suppliers.

8.5 Improvement

8.5.1 Continual improvement

The organization does not continually improve the effectiveness of the quality management system through the use of the quality policy, quality objectives, audit results, analysis of data, corrective and preventive actions, and/or management review.

8.5.2 Corrective action

The organization does not take action to eliminate the cause of nonconformities in order to prevent recurrence.

Corrective actions are not appropriate to the effects of the nonconformities encountered.

A documented procedure is not established to define requirements for:

(a) reviewing nonconformities (including customer complaints);
(b) determining the causes of nonconformities;
(c) evaluating the need for action to ensure that nonconformities do not recur;
(d) determining and implementing action needed;
(e) keeping records of the results of action taken; and
(f) reviewing corrective action taken.

8.5.3 Preventive action

The organization does not determine action to eliminate the causes of potential nonconformities in order to prevent their occurrence.

Preventive actions are not appropriate to the effects of the potential problems.

A documented procedure is not established to define requirements for:

(a) determining potential nonconformities and their causes;
(b) evaluating the need for action to prevent occurrence of nonconformities;
(c) determining and implementing action needed;
(d) keeping records of results of action taken; and
(e) reviewing preventive action taken.

See chapter 14 for how to further improve the value-adding contribution of nonconformities.

CHAPTER 11

The Closing Meeting

THIS IS NOT LIKE THE OPENING MEETING

Opening meetings are usually uneventful, but the same cannot be said of the closing meeting. If certification is essential for a big order or a major contract is at stake, the management team is likely to be boisterous in its defense of any findings that might place such business at risk.

Auditors should not rush this meeting or give the impression that they are in a hurry. Such an attitude causes concern amongst auditees and can give them the impression that the team has doubts or reservations about its audit findings.

THE AGENDA OF THE CLOSING MEETING

Auditors agree that the following subjects should be covered at the closing meeting:

- Introductions
- Compliments
- The disclaimer
- Overview
- Detailed findings
- Agreement on the need for corrective action
- The recommendation
- The report process
- Dealing with questions

Lead auditors may need to explain that it is normal protocol for them to chair the meeting. It is sensible to remember that as one is on someone else's site, there may be certain cultures or protocols to be observed (for example, no one sits in the Managing Director's chair).

Regardless of what happens, the audit team:

- must not argue amongst themselves;
- must not make inappropriate remarks; and
- must not change their minds without due cause.

If necessary, the team may choose to take a short break to discuss issues together; this is acceptable as long as it is not a frequent event.

THE INTRODUCTION

Often more people attend the closing meeting than the opening meeting, especially if things have gone well. There may be fewer people present if things have gone badly!

It is necessary to reintroduce the audit team, and if there are not too many people from the organization they might introduce themselves as well. It is normal protocol to pass around an attendance list.

COMPLIMENTS

While it is good manners to compliment the organization, this should be done appropriately and not in an exaggerated or patronizing way. If the audit team has not been made welcome, then do not lie. Perhaps, in such circumstances, it might be appropriate to say, "We would like to thank you for allowing us to complete the audit of your organization."

If particular people in the organization have been helpful, make a point of naming them and thanking them individually for their support.

THE DISCLAIMER

The audit is a sampling process. No audit team can state that there are no nonconformities; nor can the team say that the only nonconformities that exist are the ones that have been found during the audit.

Thus it is necessary to state that fact at the start of the closing meeting. For example, the auditor can say: "We would like to remind you that 'auditing' is a sampling process and our findings therefore are based on our sample. No audit team can say that no nonconformities exist or that their findings are a total representation of the state of a system. So with that said, we will now move on to the next item on our agenda."

THE OVERVIEW

The lead auditor normally presents an overview of the audit process. For example, he or she restates the scope and objectives of the audit with a quick summary of the process to date. Areas of strength are mentioned followed by areas of concern.

If the audit has a positive outcome, the lead auditor should let the auditees know straight away—it avoids long debates later when concerns are detailed (the auditees think that they have to change the auditors' minds about the decision). If they know the outcome is positive, they are more relaxed about accepting the team's findings.

THE DETAILED FINDINGS

Each auditor presents his or her own findings. It makes more sense for the person who has found something to present it.

The sequence of the presentation is a matter of choice, but the preferred option is to follow the sequence of the standard. This allows the auditee to understand what has been covered and what is yet to be covered. However, this often means that the audit team members are up and down to present, as their sections can be from several parts of the standard.

Presenting findings to senior managers requires a degree of logic and pragmatism. There will be little warmth for an auditor who cannot present a meaningful report that offers the organization something that it did not already know.

The findings need to be expressed in terms of the objectives of the audit:

- There was a nonconformity and these are the actual or potential consequences
- There is an opportunity for improvement and these are the potential benefits
- There is evidence of a lack of effectiveness as illustrated by the level of customer complaints being worse than target

This latter finding is based on the effectiveness of the process and requires an understanding of the manner in which the organization has set its targets. There needs to be an appreciation of the internal data (for example, the historical performance of the process) and the external data (for example, customer feedback or benchmarking) and how these pieces of information are collected, analyzed, and processed in order to achieve the targets. An auditor cannot make a value-adding decision about the effectiveness of a process until there is confidence in the approach used to set the targets.

This bringing together of target setting, nonconformities, opportunities for improvement, and effectiveness is illustrated in the Figure 11.1.

As the nonconformity is presented—and this can be done directly from the computer, on an overhead projector, or from the hard copy of the

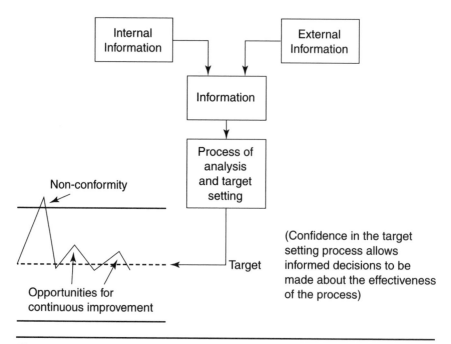

Figure 11.1 Integrating the objectives of the audit with the presentation of the findings.

forms—the auditee is asked to accept and sign the nonconformity. It is not necessary for the management team to specify the corrective action at this time, especially if there are many problems. The managers will need time to consider the nature of their responses.

It is naive to continually defer questions until the end of the audit. Managers will not sit still for an hour listening to one nonconformity after another without saying anything.

AGREEMENT ON THE NEED FOR CORRECTIVE ACTION

Although it is unrealistic to ask the management team to specify the exact nature of the corrective action to be taken, there is a minimum expectation that the need for corrective action is acknowledged. This is, by default, the inevitable consequence of the auditee's accepting the nonconformity. Additionally, the audit team and the auditee must reach an agreement on when the management team will present the corrective action plan.

As a general rule, in third-party audits, there is an expectation that follow-up audits are conducted within 13 weeks of the original audit. This tends to drive the auditee to commit to define the corrective action within the first couple of weeks.

RECOMMENDATION

The lead auditor can never tell an organization that it has met the requirements of the standard and is therefore registered to ISO 9001, or that, in a second-party audit, the organization is going to get the contract. In a third-party audit, that decision belongs to the lead auditor's governing body based on the audit team's recommendation. In a second-party audit, the decision belongs to whoever has the responsibility for placement of the contract.

Whenever a dispute arises between a lead auditor and the management team over a nonconformity or the nature of the recommendation, it is noted by the team. The decision remains unchanged, unless the audit team is clearly wrong and the management team is advised as to its next course of action, namely to appeal to the governing body or those placing the contract. This does tend to be a fruitless exercise, especially if the team has good objective evidence.

As noted in the written report, there are typically three recommendations:

- Recommend approval
- Recommend nonapproval
- Recommend approval subject to certain stated conditions

In the latter case the conditions might include the closure of certain minor nonconformities either at a subsequent follow-up visit or, as is more likely, at the next scheduled surveillance visit.

The lead auditor should formally close the meeting to avoid everyone's sitting around wondering if they can stand up and go or not.

THE REPORT PROCESS

Some auditors are able, because of their organizational skills and technological support, to produce the report for the organization before they leave the site. This is not essential. As long as copies of the nonconformity reports are left with the management team after the closing meeting, the auditor can take the next couple of days to prepare the report. It should certainly be delivered to the organization within two weeks.

It is important during the planning stage to understand who is to receive copies of the report. It is normally the audit team, whoever commissioned the audit, and the auditee.

The route of the original nonconformity reports is interesting. After being signed by the management team, they are copied and the originals are retained by the audit team. The originals are sent by the audit team to the organization's nominated representative with the audit report, the audit team retaining a copy. When the auditee has completed those, the auditee returns the originals to the auditor and retains a copy showing the corrective action taken. After the follow-up audit, the auditor completes the follow-up section and makes a copy for the auditee. The original is filed by the auditor.

The parties follow this convoluted process because each time a transaction takes place a signature is required (that is, to record the nonconformity, to agree to it, to confirm the corrective action, and to confirm the suitability and effectiveness of the corrective action). If an alternative can be agreed upon (for example, electronic completion of the forms), that makes the process much simpler. The need for signatures suggests a distrustful relationship, rather than a partnership.

The governing body of the third-party organization reviews the reports and recommendations of the lead auditor and allocates a registration number and certificate in due course. The certificate is typically valid for three years and technically remains the property of the registrar, which allows the registrar to retrieve it at any time (for example, if the organization continually fails to meet the necessary level of compliance).

DEALING WITH QUESTIONS

The auditors' capacity to deal with questions is greatly enhanced if the following criteria are established:

- Clarity of the nonconformity
- Indisputable objective evidence
- Agreement during the audit of the finding

The confidence with which the team, and particularly the lead auditor, deals with questions is a consequence of the factors just listed and of the following:

- Knowledge that a good job was done
- Experience dealing with managers at senior levels
- Knowledge of the standard and the organization's system

THINGS THAT CAN GO WRONG

Most difficulties at closing meetings come down to a lack of evidence to support a finding. If the evidence exists, there are fewer problems. However, so that you may consider some contingency plans, here is a selection of problems that auditors may encounter at the closing meeting.

- The management team does not show up for the meeting
- The managers ask how much it will cost to buy the certificate
- The audit team is asked to pose for a photograph with a replicate certificate
- The quality manager asks that one of the nonconformities be withdrawn because a new procedure has been originated since it was found
- The lead auditor is asked to exclude the requirements where nonconformities have been detected from the scope of the audit
- The management team refuses to accept a nonconformity
- Someone has a heart attack during the meeting
- The meeting starts so late that the team may not catch its plane
- When the audit team enters the room, the managers are having a violent argument
- The consultant who designed the system is present at the closing meeting and argues with all the nonconformities
- The quality manager is threatened with dismissal during the closing meeting
- There are continuous interruptions
- There is a fire emergency during the closing meeting
- The audit team is offered company T-shirts
- A manager spills a pot of coffee over the team's audit report and nonconformity reports
- The auditor is asked to show the question on the checklist that was asked during the audit to see if there was any chance that the question was misunderstood
- An auditor's findings are proved to be wrong
- The management team occupies every other seat in the meeting room so that the audit team cannot sit together
- The audit team has prepared an electronic presentation and the equipment fails
- The managing director begins by making a presentation that lasts for 45 minutes

- The human resources manager informs the lead auditor that a complaint of sexual harassment has been made about one of the audit team
- The managing director asks the auditors to provide guidance on how a nonconformity should be corrected

CHAPTER 12

Corrective Action

WHAT IS CORRECTIVE ACTION?

Corrective action is responding to an identified nonconformity to determine the root cause of a problem and beginning the process of correcting it to prevent its recurrence. This should not be confused with the "quick fix"—if an issue was an isolated incident that was able to be corrected effortlessly and was unlikely to reoccur (or even if it did it would be an inconvenience rather than a problem), then a nonconformity report was probably not justified in the first place.

There are many misunderstandings about corrective action when it is put in the context of the audit process. Traditionally, it relates to the definition just given and the term *corrective* indicates that something is wrong. However, if we take a more positive view of the audit process and put it in the context of the objectives of improvement—conformity and effectiveness—and change the term *corrective* to *responsive,* we achieve several benefits:

- The auditee company puts up less resistance, because it does not feel that it has to defend itself
- We can now accommodate opportunities for improvement rather than just the rectification of problems
- We can move auditors away from the "need" to get that first nonconformity and toward a desire to add value to the business processes

Having said that, we have to be realistic and recognize that this proactive concept is probably too much, too soon for the majority of auditors and assessment bodies. Auditees will remain, for the foreseeable future, content to hide everything that they think might be perceived as a nonconformity, and auditors will content themselves with trivial, negative reporting about calibration and document control.

Yet corrective action is a real plus in the audit process. Indeed, without it the audit process becomes a bureaucratic exercise adding no value and actually wasting resources.

It is prudent therefore that auditors and auditees give consideration to their mutual understanding of what they expect from the audit process and how they can optimize the value-adding contribution of the corrective action mechanism.

THE CORRECTIVE ACTION PROCESS: AGREEING ON THE NEED FOR CORRECTIVE ACTION (STEP 1)

The corrective action process must begin with both parties agreeing that there is a need for corrective action. This acceptance must not be a superficial response to the symptom identified but should be a true focus on the root cause of the problem and the "escape route" through which the problem slipped. Many organizations focus corrective action on attacking the root cause and forget that their existing controls failed to detect the problem.

It is a poor show when problems have to be highlighted during the internal or, even worse, the external audit process. It means that existing controls are inadequate or have not been applied as they should have been.

The simplistic techniques for identifying root causes of problems (for example, the fishbone diagram and "board blasting," the technique formally known as brainstorming) create an illusion that progress has been made toward resolution. In reality they have just got a few people excited and provided them an opportunity to get a few things off their chest. Without a structured application of investigation and data analysis, such team-based techniques can be frustrating and actually take up a lot of time eliminating "unreal" causes.

It is also simplistic to think that there is always only one root cause. For a particular occasion, there may indeed be a single root cause, but it is not the only potential cause, and this is where the fishbone type of analysis is useful as it can allow a team to identify other possibilities. The question has to be: How does the organization allocate resources to the elimination of potential causes? Here we enter two schools of thought:

- All potential causes should be eliminated
- It is not cost-effective to eliminate all potential causes

The particular school with which one aligns oneself determines the extent of one's devotion to preventing things from going wrong.

What is quite obvious is that after something has gone wrong, most organizations are able to identify what could have been done to have prevented the problem; ipso facto, all problems can be prevented. The real skill is identifying all the potential causes.

This line of thinking is essential if the audit process is to be a powerful approach to the continual improvement of a business activity. Auditees cannot console themselves with addressing the symptom; they must eliminate the most immediate root cause and then reexamine their preventive thinking to see if there are other potential causes that remain unidentified. Auditees should also conduct a rigorous examination of the preventive techniques being used to see if they can be refined to prevent similar omissions in the future. Failure mode and effects analysis (FMEA) is a classic example of where the technique is valuable but the application is weak. Used correctly, FMEA can be a powerful approach to identifying, prioritizing, and eliminating potential causes of problems. In too many organizations it is a paperwork exercise done to meet the need of some inconsiderate customer!

Corrective action cannot be viewed as the end of the process; neither can the follow-up audit. There is a wealth of activity beyond this stage of the process where true improvement can be discovered. This is uncharted territory for many auditors and auditees, but it offers genuine salvation in the pursuit of continual improvement. So when we suggest that the first step in the corrective action process is acceptance of the need for corrective action, it is in this context that we are defining the term *corrective*.

There will be critics of this thinking, and if the quality of the nonconformities remains at its current trivial level, those critics will be justified. For this level of analysis and response cannot be devoted to trivia, but only to the real issues that will add value to the business.

Improve the value-adding contribution of the nonconformity, and the resources devoted to corrective action become assigned to important business improvements.

Auditors need to revisit the plan-do-check-act cycle when searching for value-adding findings. It is rarely in *how* things are done that auditors will identify breakthrough improvements; it is in the *why* and in the "interrelationship" of activities that true value-adding contributions lie. It is in the integrity of the planning process, rather than the deployment; in the robustness of the measurement and learning processes rather than improvements in areas of trivia (for example, raising a nonconformity that states, "Five purchase orders were not signed" is likely to trigger a corrective action of "The five purchase orders are now signed"). A finding that states, "The organization has not evaluated the use of purchase orders for effectiveness" is likely to make the auditee ask, "Why do we use purchase orders? How could we eliminate the use of purchase orders?" Now we have real corrective action that adds value to the business—the solution may not only eliminate the possibility of there ever again being a nonconformity for unsigned purchase orders, but it may allow the organization to rethink its allocation of resources by finding an alternative and more cost-effective method of communicating the organization's requirements to its suppliers. This is what executives want from an audit process—the opportunity to think outside the box, challenge existing approaches, and become more cost-effective, improving productivity and achieving conformity of output in less time than they did before. Preach that in the auditor training courses, and we will have more chance of getting "buy in" from senior managers.

There is a problem, however. Most auditors cannot do what we've just described. They lack the necessary training, skill, experience, and knowledge. So for the time being, we consultants will continue to charge more than the auditors!

Can we really expect organizations to pay for the privilege of being told that something is wrong, without being given any direction on how to put it right? We have thus established the first step in the process: accept the need for corrective action.

THE AUDITEE'S RESPONSIBILITY (STEP 2)

Ownership of the solution has to lie with the auditee organization's management team. Therefore, they need to determine an effective solution or combination of solutions to prevent the problem from ever happening again. If auditors were to apply the rule of "preventing recurrence" rigidly, it would be interesting to see how many corrective action plans would be found to be effective.

It is not the purpose here to define an approach to solving problems; there are many other sources for that topic. However, the following checklist may serve useful in establishing the integrity of solutions that have been proposed to eliminate a problem found during the audit:

- Is the problem clearly defined?
- Has the problem been quantified (number of units, costs, and so on)?
- Has some containment action been taken (for example, on work in progress, units already in service, raw materials not yet used)?
- How did the organization determine who were the right people to investigate the problem?
- Have the source of the problem and other potential sources been identified and addressed?

- Have the escape routes been identified and addressed?
- Was benchmarking of best-in-class processes used to identify solutions more quickly?
- Has the organization developed a plan to implement the changes?
  - Does the plan include the following?
    - Communication with all stakeholders during the development of the solution, when it is implemented, and when it is confirmed to have been effective
    - Training
    - Testing the effectiveness of the solution over a sufficient time period
    - Modification to procedures, instructions, and training materials
    - Contingencies for overcoming resistance to the proposed solution
    - Ongoing controls
    - An update of the analysis of preventive thinking
    - A time frame for the transition of the changes to the operational personnel
- Can the organization demonstrate a mastery over the process by turning the problem on and off?
- Has the problem been "mistake-proofed"? If not, is the process audited?
- Does the organization show an understanding of reversible and irreversible remedies?
- Have other applications of the solution been exploited?
- Have those involved in the resolution been recognized?

AGREEING ON CORRECTIVE ACTION TIME FRAMES (STEP 3)

Again, the quantity, nature, and extent of the nonconformities and the complexity of the solutions influence the time frames for corrective action. As a general rule, corrective action should not go beyond a 13-week time frame. Auditors should discourage instantaneous proposals of corrective action and corresponding time frames at the closing meeting, unless the solution is obvious. It is much better for the management team to reflect on the nature and extent of the nonconformity prior to implementing a solution.

A follow-up visit is not always an additional date in the overall program. It may be set to coincide with the next scheduled surveillance visit.

SELF-VERIFICATION OF THE EFFECTIVENESS AND SUSTAINABILITY OF THE CORRECTIVE ACTION (STEP 4)

It is always sensible for the auditee to audit the effectiveness and sustainability of the corrective action before inviting the auditor to come back for the follow-up visit.

NOTIFYING THE AUDITOR (STEP 5)

Once the auditee organization has self-verified the effectiveness and sustainability of the corrective action, it can notify the auditor that the follow-up visit can take place.

VERIFYING THE IMPLEMENTATION, EFFECTIVENESS, AND SUSTAINABILITY OF THE SOLUTION (STEP 6)

The wording of this section's title is intentionally protracted to illustrate the scope of the responsibility of the auditor when determining the nature of the corrective action.

There are three distinct stages:

- The corrective action has been implemented
- The corrective action is effective
- The corrective action will continue to be effective

The manner in which the auditor verifies the three stages can vary and is determined by the nature and extent of the nonconformity. Verification methods include the following:

- Acceptance of a written response (for example, if a report was prepared that covered all the topics in our checklist given earlier in this chapter, the auditor may decide it is unnecessary to revisit the organization and verify the corrective action personally). In highly technical solutions this might be appropriate.
- Acceptance of submitted evidence. For example, if, from a sample of 15 pieces of equipment, one was found to be a week overdue, this may be minor, but it requires correcting. The system is inherently acceptable, but there was one lapse. The auditor might be prepared to accept a copy of the calibration certificate and not revisit the company. Such a response would not be acceptable if there were several pieces of equipment that had missed their calibration date.

- A revisit to the organization to verify the implementation, effectiveness, and sustainability of the corrective action (for example, where neither of the previous options is suitable or there are many actions to be verified).

Sometimes it is not the initial problem that justifies a revisit but the corrective action. For example, if the auditee states the corrective action as, "All operators who were not wearing their safety shoes have been fired," this might cause grave concern for the auditors as the company has not addressed the root cause of the nonconformity.

FORMAL CLOSURE OF THE NONCONFORMITY (STEP 7)

In the best-case scenario the previous steps enable the auditor to merely verify the effectiveness and sustainability of the corrective action and formally sign off on the nonconformity report. In the event the auditor does not accept the corrective action, the process goes back to step 1.

CHAPTER 13

Follow-Up and Surveillance Visits

THE PURPOSE OF THE FOLLOW-UP VISIT

Auditors use follow-up to verify the implementation, effectiveness, and sustainability of the corrective action. The date of the follow-up is arrived at by mutual agreement, but is unlikely to go beyond 13 weeks. In the case of an initial audit for the purpose of certification, it is in the auditee's best interests to implement and verify the corrective action quickly because failure to do so may delay the issuance of the certificate.

As has been shown in chapter 12, a site visit is not always required to verify the implementation, effectiveness, and sustainability of the corrective action; written responses or the submission of objective evidence may be accepted.

The timing of the follow-up visit, albeit subject to mutual agreement, is often determined by the availability of resources in the auditor's organization. As there are insufficient auditors to conduct all the audits, follow-up visits, and surveillance visits, it has become increasingly popular to merge the follow-up visits with a scheduled surveillance visit.

Follow-up visits usually occur when:

- a major nonconformity has been detected;
- multiple nonconformities have been detected;
- corrective action cannot be verified by any other means; or
- the nature of the corrective action gives cause for concern.

AGREEING ON THE LOGISTICS OF THE FOLLOW-UP VISIT

Unless many nonformities were raised, it is unusual for a follow-up visit to involve more than one member of the original audit team. As long as the auditor selected to do the follow-up understands the nature and extent of the nonconformity, this should not present any difficulty.

In addition to the administrative and logistical arrangements that have to be made (for example, date, time, program of meetings, personnel to be involved), ground rules must be defined:

- The follow-up concentrates on the nonconformities.
- Additional changes made to the system since the initial audit cannot be introduced for verification.
- The auditor will not be reauditing the system.
- The auditee should have already verified the implementation, effectiveness, and sustainability of the corrective action.
- The follow-up is not a consultancy visit.
- The auditor can only advise the organization of the recommendation that will be made to the governing body of the auditor's organization or whoever commissioned the audit. There can be no immediate issuing of a certificate; indeed, that may take several weeks.

EQUITY OF THE FOLLOW-UP VISIT

The follow-up visit is not another audit of the entire system; it is a verification of the implementation, effectiveness, and sustainability of the corrective action taken in response to nonconformities raised during the original audit. It is unreasonable for the auditor to begin raising new nonconformities during a follow-up visit. But what if the auditor discovers a serious problem? A nonconformity has to be raised. The difference here must be that the auditor discovered the nonconformity without using normal investigative methods; in other words, the auditor was not looking to find something new.

REPORTING THE FINDINGS OF THE FOLLOW-UP VISIT

Figures 13.1, 13.2, and 13.3 show the completed nonconformity reports and the overview, which brings the audit to an end.

AUDIT REPORT			No.: 0127a	
COMPANY	XYZ plc		DATE	06/01/2001

KEY PERSONNEL	AUDIT TEAM
J. Smyth—Chief Executive A. Button—Manufacturing Director M. Reece—Quality Manager A. Crabbe—Design Manager J. Rushmore—Production Manager	Brighton Projects Inc. P. Perfect—Lead Auditor
AUDIT STANDARD	ISO 9001:2000

REPORT	1 of 2

OVERVIEW

Scope: Design, development, and manufacture of special purpose pneumatic drive systems.

Objectives: To follow up on the findings of the original audit performed on 01/02/2001 and to determine the implementation, effectiveness, and sustainability of the corrective action taken.

Audit Findings:

Date of Audit: 06/01/2001
Location: Chipping Down, Hants

The company has taken a positive attitude to the corrective action of the nonconformities raised during the original audit.

Both of the original nonconformities have been satisfactorily addressed.

Conclusion:

Based on the original audit findings and the findings of the follow-up visit, the system does comply with the requirements of the standard ISO 9001:2000 and is effective in ensuring that products and services meet specified requirements.

Recommendation:

It is recommended that the company be given certification to the standard for the scope shown above.

Signed: P. Perfect—Lead Auditor   06/01/2001   Signed: J. Smyth—Chief Executive

Figure 13.1   Audit report.

NONCONFORMITY REPORT		No.: 0127/1
COMPANY	XYZ plc	

DEPARTMENT	Design and Development	DATE	02/01/2001

AUDIT STANDARD	ISO 9001:2000

State the finding including the objective evidence:

Process controls do not include the identification of skills and the training needs for project design staff. As a result three contracts have been lost due to the new product introduction time quoted by XYZ plc.

Process procedure DC 016A—Design and Development planning is in draft, but this does not address the skills requirement.

ISO 9001 Requirement	6.2.2 (a)	MAJOR / ~~MINOR~~	delete N/A

State the nonconformity:

The organization has not identified the necessary competence for project design staff.

AUDITOR	S. Brown	COMPANY REPRESENTATIVE	A. Crabbe

CORRECTIVE ACTION

A complete review of all current and expected future projects has been conducted and the core competencies identified. These have been incorporated into the job descriptions of the design staff.

An agenda item has been included in the management review process to ensure that the competencies of all functions are considered on an annual basis. Additionally, the project planning checklist now includes a provision for the review of competencies of all staff.

TARGET DATE	05/01/2001	SIGNED: AC	

FOLLOW-UP FINDINGS

The corrective action has addressed the immediate problem within the design area but has also addressed current and future potential recurrences in all functions. The addition of the reviews during project planning was witnessed for the new TC6754 project, and the management review agenda included an item for an evaluation of competencies based on current and expected projects.

On this basis, the nonconformity is considered closed.

DATE:	06/01/2001	SIGNED:	P. Perfect

Figure 13.2 Noncomformity report (major) showing corrective action and follow up.

NONCONFORMITY REPORT			No.: 0127/2	
COMPANY	XYZ plc			
DEPARTMENT	No. 3 Assembly Area		DATE	02/01/2001
AUDIT STANDARD		ISO 9001:2000		

State the finding including the objective evidence:

Document control—Workshop Drawings
Two of the workshop drawings examined were found to be at the wrong issue level.
Valve drive mechanism 02-0875-027 Issue G should be Issue K.
Pump case 11-1275-001 Issue B should be Issue C.
The amount of scrap caused by these two errors has been £14,000.

ISO 9001 Requirement			
State the nonconformity:	4.2.3 (g)	~~MAJOR~~ / MINOR	delete N/A

Procedures for the control of documents have not prevented the unintended use of obsolete documents.

AUDITOR	J. Bull	COMPANY REPRESENTATIVE	J. Rushmore

CORRECTIVE ACTION

All drawings within the company were audited, and all obsolete documents have been removed. A master list has been created showing all drawings and specifications and their revision level. This is held centrally on the computer. A distribution list has been prepared for all drawings to facilitate the withdrawal and reissue of documents, and a signed receipt has been introduced for acknowledging the issue of new drawings and the removal of obsolete documents. A documents officer was appointed at the beginning of this financial year with the overall responsibility of managing this process.

TARGET DATE	05/02/2001	SIGNED: JC	

FOLLOW-UP FINDINGS

The new process and appointee have clearly addressed the issue of any other obsolete documents that were in the system and have taken reasonable measures to ensure that the problem is not repeated. Fifteen drawings were taken at random and were found to be in the locations specified and at the correct issue level. The two drawings found on the original audit were also found to be correct. The organization is also looking at introducing an online system to prevent the need for hard copies of drawings, and the feasibility study for this will be completed in September 2001. All authorized drawings are stamped in red ink "original document," and notices have been placed in strategic places advising people that only drawings so marked can be used and to check the master list before use to ensure the drawing is at the correct issue level. Several auditees were interviewed and understood the process. On this basis the nonconformity is closed.

DATE:	06/01/2001	SIGNED:	P. Perfect

Figure 13.3 Nonconformity report (minor).

THE PURPOSE OF SURVEILLANCE VISITS

A surveillance visit occurs approximately every six months and addresses 20 to 30 percent of the system. These visits are to verify the continuing implementation and effectiveness of the quality management system.

Most organizations and markets are dynamic. As such, an organization's quality systems need to be responsive to prevailing circumstances and reflect the objectives and activities of the organization at any moment in time. Internal audit programs often fall into disrepair, and the external surveillance visit can be a shock to the organization's management team when it finds out that its system no longer reflects the nature of the organization's business.

If the system reflects the dynamic nature of the business and the organization's audit and review processes are strong, surveillance visits are a formality. Unfortunately this is not often the situation. The surveillance visit is used to ensure that the company is continually improving its quality system and realigning it with business objectives.

As the certification of the quality managment system is valid for three years, it is usual to attempt to complete a full systems audit during the initial certification audit and then redo the system over the next three years. Some certification bodies have a different time frame than this. The final audit of the third year and the renewal certification audit (the start of the next three years) are often merged. This is more a commercial decision to prevent the organization from going to another certification body.

Unless a serious nonconformity exists that compromises the integrity of the product, it is normal to schedule the follow-up visit to coincide with the next surveillance visit. This is also a resource issue for the certification bodies.

TO ANNOUNCE OR NOT TO ANNOUNCE

Internal audits should always be announced; to do otherwise can cause political problems within the business. Second-party surveillance visits are usually announced as that enables both organizations to resolve the logistical arrangements required. Third-party surveillance visits are also usually announced, but this is a controversial issue.

Stance one is that surveillance visits should be unannounced to ensure that the organization does not have its people running around tying labels on everything, creating the perfect world for the day of the audit. In other words, allow the auditor to see the company as it really is. Against this view are the logistical problems that unannounced visits can create and the impression such visits give of a policing approach rather than the partnering approach that auditors should try to foster.

Stance two is that surveillance visits should be announced, allowing the parties sufficient time to plan a meaningful audit, where both parties are suitably prepared.

A neutral option is that the auditor reserves the right to make unannounced visits, perhaps using this approach sparingly. The questions are "why?" and "when?"

If nonconformities are discovered in a company during scheduled and announced surveillance visits, what advantage does an unannounced audit offer? If a company never has a nonconformity, making an unannounced visit might create the impression that the auditor is determined to find a nonconformity and has chosen a covert method for doing so.

Surprisingly some organizations actually ask for unannounced audits! Unannounced visits may be initiated when:

- there has been a major reorganization of the auditee's company (for example, a merger or takeover);
- there is doubt about the integrity of the auditee's product quality; or
- the organization has modified its range of products or processes (for example, a change in scope).

If the unannounced audit is chosen, be prepared to sit in reception for a long time!

THE DOS AND DON'TS OF SURVEILLANCE VISITS

It is good practice to involve people in the surveillance visit who have not been involved previously (for example, new employees). This ensures the continuity of the quality management system. It also makes sense to refer back to areas of concern discovered during previous audits to ensure that the corrective action continues to be effective.

Do examine internal audit reports and the outputs of the management review process, as these are the internal methods of determining if the quality system is effective.

It is necessary to originate a report and, if need be, nonconformity reports, following the processes for raising such findings and implementing corrective actions discussed earlier.

Things to be avoided are the habitual examination of training records, calibration records, and document control. These are not more important than other requirements in ISO 9001:2000 and therefore do not have to be checked at every surveillance visit.

CHAPTER 14

The Future of Auditing

THE PARADIGM SHIFT: SETTING A NEW EXAMPLE

In the next five years auditing must realize a paradigm shift in approach. The emphasis of the audit must be on genuine improvement, aligned with business objectives, not on trivial nonconformities. This change is required both by auditors and management representatives in auditee organizations.

Resources cannot be devoted separately to quality, environmental, and safety audits; these must be integrated, which requires extensive training of auditors in new areas of expertise.

The methods of auditing cannot concentrate on conformity alone but must put greater emphasis on effectiveness and continual improvement. Auditors must spend less time examining how things are done and more time on why they are done and how they are integrated with other business processes.

The caliber of auditors must improve and go beyond the standard of the mediocre former quality manager. For this to happen, certification bodies will have to be prepared to spend more money to get the right people.

There is no reason why an external auditor cannot lead a team of internal auditors in a more rigorous audit of the quality system twice a year. This requires the trust of both parties, but it does offer an excellent approach for improving the overall effectiveness of the audit process.

Integrating audits against ISO 9001 and assessments for national quality or excellence awards is another opportunity. But, then, assessors of the latter might not lower themselves to the mediocrity and uninteresting evaluation of ISO 9001 implementation!

SELF-ASSESSMENT

Certification bodies and auditees may agree on a scoring method to identify areas of improvement and areas in accordance with the standard, rather than just relying on positive and negative reporting. An example of such a method is presented here.

ISO 9001:2000 Self-Assessment

Complete each question by scoring your organization as follows:

5 = Strongly agree; 4 = Agree; 3 = Neither agree nor disagree; 2 = Disagree; 1 = Strongly disagree.

If a question is not applicable do not score it and reduce the number of questions in the calculation for the section by the number of questions marked N/A.

Section 1 General Requirements

	5	4	3	2	1
1. We have clear evidence of continual improvement of the quality management system.					
2. We understand our business processes and how they interact with each other.					
3. All our processes are planned, monitored, controlled, and improved continually.					
4. Outsourced processes are controlled.					

Total points Section 1		A
Number of questions applicable		B
A/B *%		

Section 2 Documentation Requirements					
	5	4	3	2	1
5. Our quality system includes a meaningful policy and measurable objectives.					
6. Our quality manual and procedures add value to the business.					
7. The records we keep ensure compliance with legislation.					
8. The scope of our system is understood by everyone.					
9. Our system prevents the use of obsolete documents.					
10. Our records are easily retrievable.					

Total points Section 2		C
Number of questions applicable		D
C/D *%		

Section 3 Management Responsibility	5	4	3	2	1
11. By their actions, it is easy to identify top management's support.					
12. Top management is genuinely interested in customer satisfaction in the system.					
13. The quality policy and how it relates to one's job is understood by everyone.					
14. Everyone understands their objectives in the context of quality requirements.					
15. There is a strong quality-planning process.					
16. The system remains effective even during reorganizational changes.					
17. Everyone has a clear line of responsibility and authority.					
18. The management representative has appropriate authority.					
19. Internal communications are effective and timely.					
20. The management review process is an effective evaluation of the effectiveness of the system and drives continual improvement.					
Total points Section 2		E			
Number of questions applicable		F			
E/F *%					

Section 4 Resource Management	5	4	3	2	1
21. All employees do their job competently.					
22. Competency needs are identified and appropriate training is provided.					
23. Training is evaluated for effectiveness.					
24. Training records are maintained.					
25. The buildings, equipment, and work space is suitable to do a good job.					
26. The work environment is suitable and safe.					

Total points Section 4		G
Number of questions applicable		H
G/H *%		

Section 5 Project Planning

	5	4	3	2	1
27. We understand the quality objectives and requirements for our products/services.					
28. We implement effective process controls to ensure that the product/service is acceptable.					
29. Our records demonstrate that products and processes are acceptable.					

Total points Section 5		I
Number of questions applicable		J
I/J * %		

Section 6 Customer Management	5	4	3	2	1
30. We have effective processes for understanding customer requirements.					
31. We have effective processes for understanding legal requirements relating to our products.					
32. Our review of customer requirements is completed prior to our agreeing to supply.					
33. We do not undertake to supply things that we cannot deliver.					
34. There is always documentary evidence of what a customer stated as its requirements.					
35. We manage changes to customer requirements professionally.					
36. We handle all customer communications very well.					

Total points Section 6		K
Number of questions applicable		L
K/L *%		

Section 7 Design and Development

	5	4	3	2	1
37. We have effective design and development planning processes.					
38. There are clear responsibilities during the design and development process.					
39. We maintain up-to-date design plans.					
40. We consider all appropriate internal and external sources of information during design and development.					
41. Our design drawings and/or specifications provide all the information required to produce and test our products.					
42. The right people get involved, at the right time, in the design review process.					
43. We verify designs prior to the commitment of production resources.					
44. We validate that the product meets user needs.					
45. We effectively manage design changes/modifications.					

Total points Section 6		M
Number of questions applicable		N
M/N *%		

Section 8 Purchasing					
	5	4	3	2	1
46. We adequately control our suppliers.					
47. We apply criteria to the selection of our suppliers.					
48. We reevaluate our suppliers, and they improve continuously.					
49. We have an effective process for placing orders with customers.					
50. We have effective checks to ensure that purchased product meets our requirements.					

Total points Section 8		O	
Number of questions applicable		P	
O/P *%			

Section 9 Controlling Production Processes

	5	4	3	2	1
51. Our production processes are suitably controlled.					
52. We control the output of all our production processes.					
53. We have effective controls for product identification and traceability.					
54. Material supplied by our customers is controlled effectively.					
55. Handling/storage/packaging/delivery prevents damage to or deterioration of the product.					
56. All relevant equipment is suitably calibrated.					

Total points Section 9		Q
Number of questions applicable		R
Q/R *%		

Section 10 Measurement, Analysis, and Improvement	5	4	3	2	1
57. We have effective processes for continual improvement.					
58. We measure and respond to customer satisfaction data.					
59. We have an effective internal audit process that leads to meaningful improvements.					
60. Process measurement ensures the effective operation of the business.					
61. Product measurement ensures that we meet customer requirements.					
62. Product cannot be released until all specified checks have been performed.					
63. We effectively control nonconforming product.					
64. Processes for data capture and analysis lead to improvements.					
65. The quality system is improved continuously.					
66. Corrective action prevents the recurrence of problems.					
67. Preventive actions stop things from going wrong.					
Total points Section 10		S			
Number of questions applicable		T			
S/T * %					

Summary of Results		
Section	**Heading**	**%**
1	General Requirements	
2	Documentation Requirements	
3	Management Responsibility	
4	Resource Management	
5	Product Planning	
6	Customer Management	
7	Design and Development	
8	Purchasing	
9	Controlling Production Processes	
10	Measurement, Analysis, and Improvement	
Overall	Average of 1 to 10	

Radar Chart of Results (Each Circle Represents 10 Percent with Zero at the Center). For each section of questions, the corresponding score is entered on the chart.

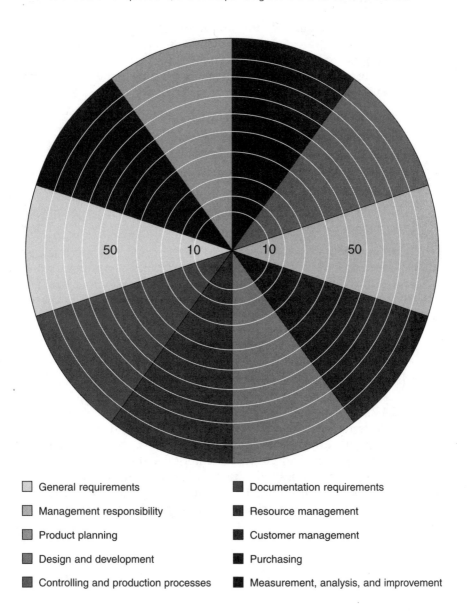

☐ General requirements	■ Documentation requirements
☐ Management responsibility	■ Resource management
☐ Product planning	■ Customer management
☐ Design and development	■ Purchasing
☐ Controlling and production processes	■ Measurement, analysis, and improvement

IMPROVING THE VALUE-ADDING CONTRIBUTION OF AUDIT REPORTS

Clearly, gaining acceptance for the new auditing approach requires auditors and auditees to agree on a strategy. It is suggested that audit checklists focus on the matrix shown in Table 14.1.

According to this approach, auditors will focus their questions on systematic issues, such as the following:

- Has the activity been planned, based on all available data and information, including benchmarking references?
- Is there evidence that the plan has been deployed consistently throughout the organization?
- What measurement and learning activities are used to determine the effectiveness of the plan and the extent of deployment?
- Is there evidence of improvement based on measurement and learning activities?

These questions can then be placed in the context of the business objectives (for example, safety, customer satisfaction, product quality, environment, costs, and knowledge management, or the other business objectives defined by the organization based on the needs and expectations of its stakeholders).

The modern approach to developing checklists will be based on the flowchart shown in Figure 14.1.

Checklists need to link the process under investigation with overall policy and strategy (clauses 5.3/5.4.1).

Checklists must then address how the organization develops its plans (clause 5.4.2).

Questions must then focus on the specific process under investigation (clause 7). Specific processes include inputs, outputs, resources, and controls, including process and product monitoring and measurement.

Following on from questions about the specific process, there may be additional questions concerning the generic requirements of the standard.

Finally, evidence of audit (clause 8.2.2) and review (clause 5.6) need to be verified.

Table 14.1 Audit checklist matrix.

	Safety	Customer	Product	Environment	Costs	Knowledge	People	Efficiency	Objectives
Plan									
Do									
Check									
Act									

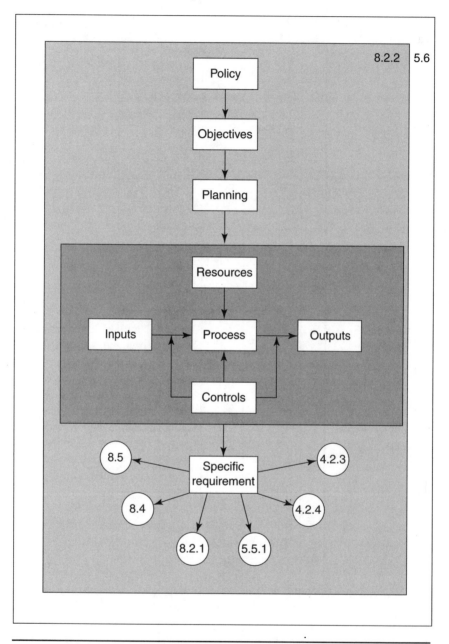

Figure 14.1   Developing meaningful checklists.

When the audit report is prepared, based on this type of questioning, it can highlight the systematic weaknesses (that is, either in the design of the system, the deployment of the system, the measurement and learning techniques used, or the absence of evidence of a systematic approach to continuous improvement) and then illustrate the impact of the nonconformity in the context of the business objectives:

- This is a potential safety hazard (safety)
- This will affect customer satisfaction (customer)
- This has resulted in higher reject levels (product quality and cost)
- This has a potentially harmful effect on the local water supply (environment)
- This has reduced the margin on the product by 2 percent (cost)
- Not providing this knowledge to sales personnel has had a negative impact on the launch of the new product (knowledge)

This combination of cause and effect is well illustrated in J. P. Russell and Terry Regel's *After the Quality Audit: Closing the Loop on the Audit Process,* 2nd ed. (ASQ Press). There the authors highlight the "reason" and the "pain" as being the basis for audit reporting.

The logic of using this type of questioning and reporting is consistent with the approach of the European Quality Foundation for Quality Management. Its approach is called RADAR (results; approach; deployment; assessment; and review). The capacity to place nonconformities in the context of business objectives and the impact on stakeholders identifies the actual or potential consequences of the problem. This is a necessary factor in value-adding reporting.

Auditors, in preparing their final report, can use the matrix shown in Table 14.2 to organize their findings.

THE IMPACT ON THE INTERNAL AUDITOR

While it is necessary for third-party auditors to realign their focus from mere compliance to adding value, it is equally important for the internal auditor to become more competent in the application of the internal audit process. Indeed, the process itself may require rethinking.

To optimize the use of resources it is probably sensible to integrate the internal audit processes (for example, environmental, safety, and quality). However, for an internal auditor to be competent in such a spectrum of disciplines requires an extensive education and training program. After all, the audit process is the same; it is the subject material that changes.

Table 14.2 Facilitating value-adding reporting.

Requirement of ISO 9001:2000	Nonconformity	Opportunity for improvement	Impact on effectiveness of the system, process, or product	Objective evidence	Specific clause of the standard	Person who agreed to the finding	Actual or potential consequences of this finding for the business
4							
5							
6							
7							
8							

Selling the need for internal auditors to top management can be tough. Getting people to "volunteer" to be auditors can be tougher! However, if the initiative is "sold" on the basis of organizational and individual development (exposing more people to more aspects of the business), a persuasive case can be built. Most internal auditors are part-time. By definition, they are part-time something else—their real job. It is important that those performing internal audits gain some recognition for their efforts. For example, if there is an appraisal process, the internal audit program manager should have an input to the auditor's appraisal as well as the auditor's line manager or principle process owner.

More consideration needs to be given to the frequency of audits. Too often some arbitrary frequency is selected without consideration of the impact of the activity on the business or the results of previous audits. The methodology shown in Table 14.3 is used in some organizations to determine audit frequencies.

The evaluation of the audit process should consider the overall nature of nonconformities to determine if there are systematic errors, such as the following:

- Lack of training
- Procedures not updated
- Organizational changes
- Poor communications
- Disciplinary issues
- Accessibility of information
- Lack of resources
- Equipment capability

Consider the desired outcome when a nonconformity is detected—corrective action. When a nonconformity is classified as "major," something gets done about it. When it is called "minor," it may or may not get resolved. If the desired outcome is the same, why categorize the nonconformities as major or minor for internal audits?

When the management review process considers these generic problems (for example, lack of training, out of date procedures, or organizational changes), efforts can be made to address the systematic weakness rather than the isolated series of incidents. This can be easily handled by using a database.

The responsibilities of internal auditors must be clear. See the job description included as Appendix E.

Table 14.3 Determining the internal audit frequency.

	1	2	3	4	5	Frequency
	Impact on business 5 = critical 1 = minor	Previous audit results 5 = many NCRs 1 = no NCRs	Turnover of staff 5 = High 1 = Low	Complexity of processes 5 = High 1 = Low	Total columns 1 x 2 x 3 x 4	> 200 = Five times per year 150 - 199 = Four times per year 101 - 149 = Three times per year 51 - 100 = Twice per year < 50 = Once per year
Process A	5	5	3	3	225	5
Process B	2	2	3	2	24	1
Process C	4	3	3	2	72	2

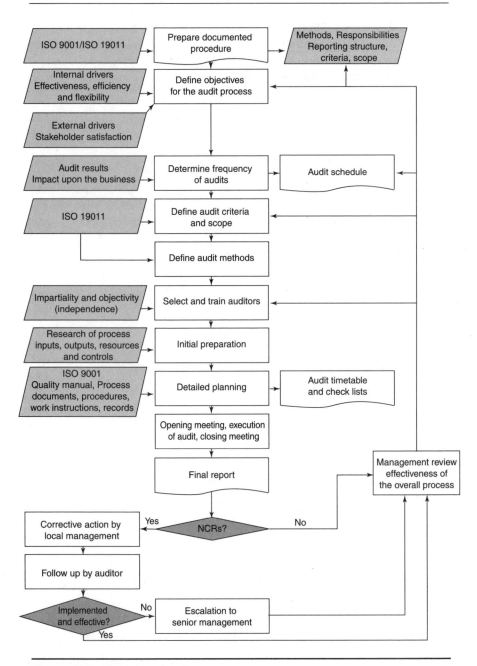

Figure 14.2 The internal audit process.

The flowchart in Figure 14.2 indicates some of the issues that the new standard addresses (ISO 9001:2000 clause 8.2.2). For internal auditing to be recognized as a value adding activity, there must be a clear process that covers not only the requirements of the standard but the needs of the business as well

Case Study One: The Business Advantages of Effective Auditing

BACKGROUND

An audit was commissioned by Molex Interconnect A.G. (the client), an organization that purchases products from outside of Europe for redistribution within Europe. The organization is based in Eindhoven, the Netherlands, and it subcontracts its transport and warehousing operations.

The original warehouse provider was audited, and many nonconformities were found. At the follow-up visit, there was little evidence that the organization had taken any corrective action, and an extension to the timetable was given. Again the follow-up visit determined that no positive corrective action had been taken, and the decision was made to cancel the contract and find another warehouse provider.

The subcontractor chosen was BAX Global Logistics BV. The transfer of the operation to the new service provider was poorly planned because of the limited time available, and for the first month, the performance indicators showed poor results. It was decided to perform an audit to determine an improvement plan.

The scope of the original audit included the following:

- The audit aimed to determine the extent of conformity of the subcontractor's system against ISO 9001, to establish the effectiveness of the system, and to identify areas for improvement.
- The location was the BAX Global Logistics BV Warehouse in Eindhoven, which employed approximately 30 people.
- The operations were the receipt, storage, picking, packing, and delivery of components in line with customer requests. Thus, the processes under investigation were as follows:
  - Goods receipt processing (inbound processing)
  - Storage of products in the warehouse
  - Picking
  - Packing/labeling
  - Shipment (outbound processing)

- The key performance indicators were as follows:
  - Inventory accuracy (target 99.9 percent; actual performance was approximately 93 percent)
  - Shipping accuracy (target 500 parts per million; actual performance was 6000 parts per million)
  - Goods receipt processing time (target 99 percent conformance to GRPT; actual was 50 percent)
  - On-time delivery performance (target 100 percent; actual performance was 85 percent)

ACKNOWLEDGMENTS

Any audit report is only as good as the actions it stimulates. These actions are not taken by the auditor but by members of the organization willing to invest their time and effort in taking the necessary corrective actions. This case study highlights a real success story, but that would not have been possible without the efforts of the following people.

Eamon McAleavey, general manager, Molex Interconnect A.G.

Lex Cleton, BAX Global Logistics BV

Reinier Remmelink, quality manager, Molex Interconnect A.G.

Ad Wijnhoven, site manager, BAX Global Logistics BV

THE AUDIT REPORT

The audit report highlighted many problems that were consistent with the initial poor planning of the operation and the misunderstanding of the complexity of the client's product range. Many process-related problems were also identified, such as the following:

- Incoming products were not packed by the manufacturing companies in accordance with the agreed-upon standard pack quantities. This meant that up to 300 man-hours per month were spent in repacking and relabeling. (See ISO 9001:2000 clause 7.4.3.)
- Because the warehouse was not being preadvised about shipments, when huge deliveries arrived from the United States or Japan the resources to process them through goods receiving were just not available. (See ISO 9001:2000 clause 6.1.)

- The layout of the warehouse did not enable a logical flow of products, and this led to confusion as to which products had been checked, repacked, or were suspect. (See ISO 9001:2000 clause 6.3.)
- Items were located based on space available, without consideration for the frequency with which they were picked, and thus some regularly picked items could be at the back of the warehouse on the top racks. This caused delays in processing time. (See ISO 9001:2000 clause 4.1[f].)
- Picking lists were barely legible because of poor print quality and inadequate lighting, and the pickers and packers had no awareness of part numbers, product descriptions, labeling requirements, and so on. As a consequence many orders were being picked incorrectly with overshipments and undershipments being a regular customer complaint. (See ISO 9001:2000 clause 6.2.2[d].)
- Many part-time people were being used who had received little training, and there was little evidence of their commitment to the organization or the level of quality expected. (See ISO 9001:2000 clause 6.2.2[d].).
- The outbound area, where packers prepared consignment orders for shipment, was poorly laid out, causing confusion about which consignments were complete. (See ISO 9001:2000 clause 6.4.)

THE CORRECTIVE ACTION PLAN

The client and BAX Global Logistics BV, developed a quality plan, based on ISO 9001, to address the situation.

As a result the following corrective actions were taken:

- The client preadvises the organization about deliveries to enable advanced resource planning.
- A system of tracking the hours spent on repacking was introduced to charge back the costs to the supplier.
- Clarification of the standard pack quantities was provided.
- The goods inwards processing area was reorganized to enable clearer identification of incoming shipments, and new work tables were purchased that divided the incoming products that had not been processed from those that had.

- An extensive training program was supported by the client. It included:
  - ISO 9001 awareness training;
  - problem solving;
  - internal auditor training;
  - product awareness training; and
  - safety training, including the production of eight in-house videos.
- The policy of using predominantly part-time staff was changed, and additional resources were provided.
- Weekly meetings were held between the client and the organization reviewing the performance metrics and the overall planning process.
- An "ABC analysis" of the stock movement was conducted so that frequently moving items were placed nearer the packing areas.
- A quarantine area was erected to enable the segregation of suspect products, thus clearing the work area. This was subsequently relocated into a much smaller part of the warehouse as the improvements reduced the number of problems.
- Bar coding and Radio Frequency scanners were introduced for picking and packing to eliminate human error.
- One hundred percent auditing was introduced for key customers after picking, packing, and labeling, and any errors were immediately fed back to the picker or packer. This has since been reduced as the increased visibility of who was involved and the other improvements reduced the number of errors.

THE SITUATION NOW

The accompanying charts show the improvements in the performance metrics.

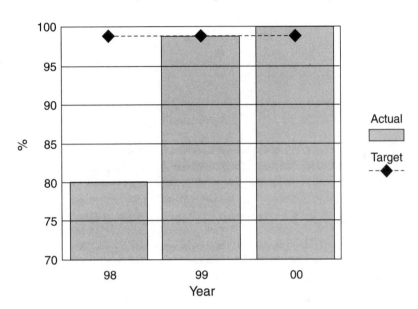

Warehouse Delivery Performance

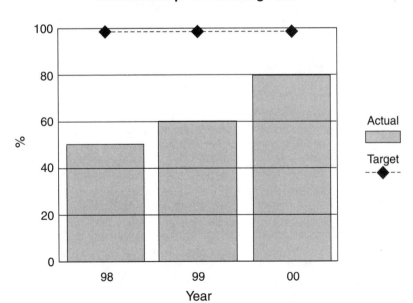

Goods Receipt Processing Time

Inventory Accuracy

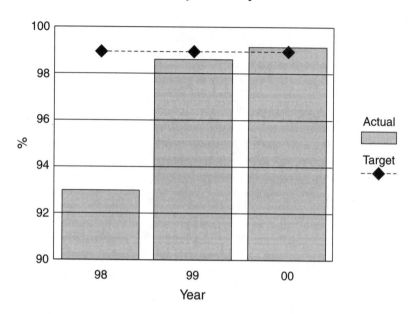

Shipping Accuracy

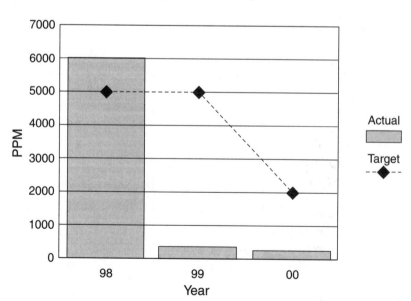

POSTSCRIPT

Extensive effort that results in success deserves recognition. This has been the case for those involved in this particular case study:

- Molex Interconnect A.G. won the European Supply Chain Award
- Eamon McAleavey is now the director of sourcing and logistics at Molex Europe
- Lex Cleton continues to provide support having sold the operation to BAX Global
- Ad Wijnhoven has successfully completed his M.B.A. and is destined for a bright future
- Reinier Remmelink will become the assistant to Eamon McAleavey and is now a recognized expert in the application of the supply chain organization reference (SCOR) model, a regular speaker at universities in the Netherlands, and the author of articles based on his work

Lessons Learned (Based on Feedback during Auditor/Lead Auditor Courses)

LESSONS LEARNED REGARDING THE OPENING MEETING

- Focus on the objective of the meeting.
- Remain professional.
- Establish the roles of those attending the meeting, and agree on the ground rules.
- Establish areas of common interest regarding the output of the audit process.
- Establish alternatives in case there are problems during the audit.
- Develop a spirit of trust and partnership.
- Remain flexible, but do not cave in to the auditee.
- Evaluate the suggestions and comments of the auditee before making a decision.
- When problems are raised get to the real issue quickly.
- Pay attention to what is being said.
- Auditors should understand when they can interrupt the meeting to assist the lead auditor.
- Be courteous at all times.
- Emphasize the reality of the situation (for example, the value of the contract).
- The lead auditor must take the initiative and lead the meeting.
- If things are getting heated or going off track, consider using an adjournment.
- The lead auditor must perceive situations quickly and respond accordingly.
- Observe the body language of the auditee's representatives.
- Be patient.
- Make sure that everyone knows the duration of the meeting at the start.
- Do not allow a climate of tension to develop.

- Remember that when the attendance list is distributed, you must get it back.
- Be prepared to make and receive a presentation.
- The auditors must work as a team and be a good example of teamwork.
- When being told people's names, be sure to write them down. Try and right them down in the same sequence as people are seated around the table so that you can use people's names.
- Respect local culture (for example, if the auditee uses titles ensure that the same respect is shown to the auditee).
- Refer to your preaudit visit as this enables the auditee's representatives to feel that you know the organization.
- Manage the time in a polite but firm manner.
- Understand the basic principles of meetings (for example, agenda, ground rules, roles, timekeeping, involvement of people).
- Expect the unexpected.
- Do not say, "When we find a nonconformity," but, "In the event that we find a nonconformity."

LESSONS LEARNED REGARDING THE EXECUTION OF THE AUDIT

- Be well prepared and have a solid plan
- The plan must allow for some flexibility and cannot be defined down to the last minute
- Avoid prejudices
- Make sure that nonconformities are understood and agreed to by the auditee
- Be aware of any previous audit findings
- Remember that the objective of the audit is to determine the extent of conformity, not the level of nonconformity
- Understand the organization's business objectives and processes
- Make sure that you are using the latest version of documents ·
- Focus on business-critical activities and not trivia
- Be careful with auditees who appear too enthusiastic to show you certain things—this can cost time
- Make detailed notes about your findings and record the numbers of equipment, revision levels of documents, results of process measures, and so on

- If necessary, ask for a moment to record your findings
- Be observant of what is happening around you, and do not be restricted to the questions on the checklist
- Remember that the second question in the audit is determined by the answer to the first question
- Do not become paranoid about getting through every question on the checklist
- Structure questions around things that the auditee understands; do not blind the auditee with terminology from ISO 9001
- Although the beginning of an interview can be informal, it must progress through discussion to a formal interview situation; it should never become an interrogation
- Use simple, one-line questions
- Demonstrate a profound understanding of the auditee's business priorities
- Persist with questions until sufficient evidence has been obtained to determine conformity, effectiveness, an opportunity for improvement, or a negative finding
- It is important that the team agree on a communications strategy to be operated during the audit
- Manage personal traits; do not get angry, excited, or aggressive
- Remember that each new interview is a new experience; just because the previous interview went badly does not mean that the auditor should enter the next interview looking for revenge
- The lead auditor must keep in touch with the other auditors during the process; so it is a good idea to schedule regular meetings together
- Learn how to deal with stress
- Prioritize what is important in the eyes of your client and of the auditee
- Although documents have to be examined, an audit cannot be done in an office; auditors need to move around the business checking products, equipment, and materials
- Always keep a "bucket list" of questions that can be used with any auditee (for example, about quality policy, objectives, responsibilities, document control, records, training)
- Never rely on hearsay; always find another way of verifying the nonconformity

LESSONS LEARNED REGARDING THE CLOSING MEETING

- Objective evidence is everything; without it you will suffer at the closing meeting.
- Avoid conflict by expressing an understanding of common ground.
- Focus on key themes.
- Do not surrender your notes for copying or any other reason—they can get shredded.
- You have to show that you know the standard and the auditee's system.
- You must be able to link between your finding, your checklist, the standard, and the organization's system.
- You must be able to explain the consequences of the nonconformity.
- Watch out for people who bring documentation to the meeting; they have reference material with which they can challenge you.
- Self-control is vital—don't let them grind you down.
- Ask questions and clarify understanding. There must be no open issues where the auditor thinks the nonconformity has been agreed to and the auditee thinks that it has been withdrawn.
- Establish the ground rules and roles.
- Create confidence by expressing issues in the context of the business objectives, illustrating the consequences of findings.
- Remember that experience is not gained overnight but can be accelerated by working with experienced people, doing role-plays, doing case studies, attending workshops, and reading books.
- Be assertive, but do not let your attitude create a perception of aggressiveness.
- Be careful with terminology (for example, avoid contradictions in the findings).
- Make sure that the presentation of findings is professional.
- Respect the organization's dress code.
- Manage the time, but do not create the impression that you want to get out of the meeting.

Case Study Two: One Approach to Developing Policy and Objectives and How They May Be Deployed

BACKGROUND

A process improvement program was commissioned by an organization. The organization had already achieved QS9000 and ISO 14000 certification. A series of improvement programs had already been initiated by the parent company (for example, statistical process control, total quality management).

An initial review of the system showed no integrated approach to process management—that is, there were too many measures, often in conflict, causing process suboptimization. The review also found a lack of clarity regarding roles and responsibilities and a major issue with resources (that is, assignment of resources to new product introduction was not commensurate with the value of new business). Little use had been made of cross-functional or intradepartmental process improvement teams, and there was no clear approach for defining priorities.

The key performance indicators were as follows:

- Inventory accuracy (target 99.9 percent; actual performance was approximately 80 percent)
- Shipping accuracy (target 1000 parts per million; actual performance 20,000 parts per million)
- New product introduction time (target 16 weeks; actual performance 40 weeks)
- On-time delivery performance (target 100 percent; actual performance was 70 percent)
- New business hit rate (target 1 in 10; actual performance 1 in 40)

THE DESIGN TEAM

The combined team of Eurospan and client representatives identified that there was:

- no organizational structure to support process improvement;
- no effective measurement of the overall approach to business process management;
- no clear ownership of processes;
- a focus on short-term issues rather than long-term solutions;
- a fragmented approach to deploying policy and strategy; and
- no integration of measures.

THE PROGRAM

- An organizational structure was established with a business lead team, project team sponsors, incremental and breakthrough cross-functional teams, within-process natural work teams, and an ideas process. This Business Lead team was required to define policy and objectives and deploy them in an integrated manner to all process owners.
- A new product introduction process team was facilitated to reduce cycle time and improve the PPM levels of products at initial launch.
- A full-time facilitator was recruited and trained and has sustained the program for more than a year since the termination of the consultancy contract.
- An integrated measurement and continual improvement process was introduced based on the Deming approach (for example, using the plan-do-check-act cycle; using daily management boards). (See W. Edwards Deming, *Out of the Crisis* [MIT Press, 2000].)
- A self-assessment program based on the European Foundation for Quality Management excellence model was introduced.

The development and deployment of policy and objectives became the driver in the business. (See Figure A.1.) The business lead team took into account internal and external data (for example, employee satisfaction survey results, performance metrics, customer satisfaction data, market trends) and used them to formulate policy and objectives.

For each element of policy, measurable objectives were determined for three to five years, and these were then "step-managed" by determining where the organization needed to be by the end of the first year.

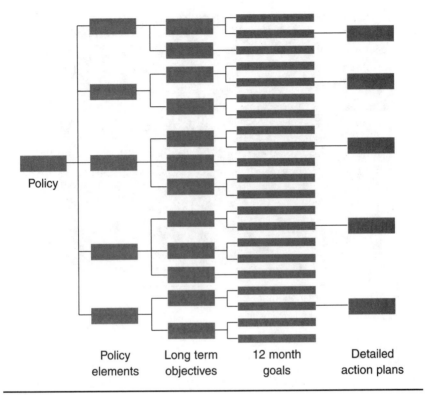

| Policy elements | Long term objectives | 12 month goals | Detailed action plans |

Figure A.1 Policy deployment.

Source: Eurospan Developments Ltd. QMS Auditor/Lead Auditor Course 2000. Used with permission.

Detailed action plans were prepared for each of these first-year goals. The goals were called *focal points* and were used by each process owner to set integrated measures for each process. The information was displayed on "daily management boards" (see Figure A.2).

THE NEW METHODOLOGY

The organization's policy and objectives have been and continue to be reviewed and refined using actual market, customer, and internal data enabling a constancy of purpose for all employees.

The daily management board links the business objectives (focal points), which are translated for each process into specific measures. These are recorded on the "Plan" line on the board. Actual performance

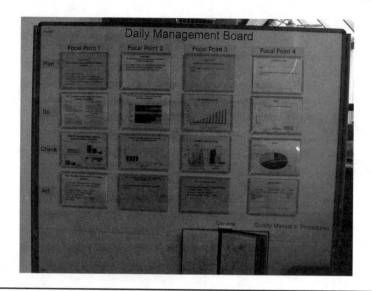

Figure A.2 A daily management board.
Picture by T. O'Flaherty. Used with permission.

against target is recorded on the "Do" line. The process owner and team review the performance and record their understanding of the performance against the "Check" line (for example, using Pareto analysis). Based on this review an action plan is established against the "Act" line.

Consistent with the Deming approach, significant work was done on leadership development (for example, a 21-day leadership training program was introduced for first-line process leaders).

The traditional inspection orientation was changed to a prevention-based approach using extensive deployment of failure mode and effects analysis, statistical process control, and *poka-yoke* techniques.

Emphasis was placed on the development of key suppliers (for example, ensuring that essential suppliers were developed to a point where they were able to self-qualify tooling, including Cpk, five-shot analysis, and gage R&R study).

A cost-of-poor-quality study was performed, which resulted in four core project teams being commissioned. The outcome of these project teams was a saving of £4 million in the first year.

A comprehensive "train the trainer" program was introduced to improve the effectiveness of on-the-job training.

There was an element of a "fear" culture in the organization and a certain emphasis on quantity over quality. To counter this, the leadership development program was supported by leadership mentoring, employee surveys, and focus groups. Process teams were given training and continual support. Within two years, 98 percent of employee satisfaction indicators were higher than the national average.

Multifunctional teams and the use of process measures relating to effectiveness, efficiency, and flexibility saw the eradication of political and interdepartmental barriers. A number of middle and senior managers did not feel comfortable with this approach and decided to leave the organization.

Objective setting and reviews were replaced by performance-related incentives on a team basis.

THE SITUATION NOW

Despite dramatic changes in market conditions, the organization has continued to make an enviable profit and has significantly reduced the level of complaints per 1000 line items shipped.

A new computer system has been fully deployed, and an intranet quality management system has been established.

Employee satisfaction measures of leadership performance have shown a dramatic improvement, and 98 percent of all employee satisfaction indicators are better than the national average, in spite of a downturn in business.

The program is fully self-sustaining with a minimum of training and consultancy input from Eurospan.

The EFQM excellence score has gained the organization accolades in the "Excellence Ireland" process. The organization has scored in excess of 600 points.

New product introduction for the biggest project in the organization's history came in on time, on cost, and with previously unequaled PPM levels.

Average natural work team savings are in the region of £12,000, and there have been more than 50 of these teams (incremental improvements). Cross-functional project teams have realized savings in excess of £5 million (breakthrough improvements).

Typical Action Plan for Implementing ISO 9001:2000

Note: The focus of implementation must be on aligning the quality management system with the needs of the business. Because of the uniqueness of each enterprise, this plan illustrates only the issues related to the standard.

Define purpose and objectives for the system.

Gain understanding of requirements.

Identify stakeholder needs.

Specify scope of the system.

Explain requirements and implications to top management.

Gain top management commitment and explain its responsibilities (clauses 5.1, 5.2, 5.3, 5.4.1, 5.4.2, 5.5.1, 5.5.2, 5.5.3, 5.6).

Assign responsibilities for project.

Identify risks and constraints and prepare contingencies.

Establish a business process model—define inputs, outputs, resources, and controls (clause 4.1).

Identify the interrelationships between processes and their impact on the achievement of business objectives (clause 4.1).

Identify and define responsibilities for process owners (clause 5.5.1).

Communicate with employees (clause 5.5.3).

Identify immediate training needs (clause 6.2).

Identify outsourced processes within the scope of the system (clause 4.1).

Prepare quality policy and objectives (clause 4.2.1).

Prepare a quality manual (clause 4.2.2).

Define necessary documentation and controls (clause 4.2.3).

Implement a documented procedure for document control (clause 4.2.3).

Prepare process documentation (clause 4.2.2).

Prepare a document master list (clause 4.2.3).

Identify mandatory and essential records (clause 4.2.3).

Prepare a list of records and define controls (clause 4.2.4).

Implement a documented procedure for the control of records (clause 4.2.4)

Clarify and communicate customer requirements to all employees (clause 5.2).

Ensure integration between quality policy and objectives and overall policy and objectives (clause 5.3).

Define a policy review process including frequency, responsibilities, data used, and records (clause 5.3).

Establish measurable objectives based on the business needs at all levels (clause 5.4.1).

Prepare overall quality plan to ensure that the system focuses on planning, control, and improvement of activities (clause 5.4.2).

Define controls to maintain system integrity during potential organizational changes (clause 5.4.2).

Define competency requirements, responsibilities, and authorities (for example, by using job descriptions) (clause 5.5.1).

Appoint and train a management representative with responsibilities as defined in clause 5.5.2.

Define company communications needs and map the necessary processes and measures of effectiveness (clause 5.5.3).

Define a process for management review, including inputs/outputs, frequency, attendance, and records (clause 5.6).

Establish a process for resource identification and integrate this with current and predicted business needs (clause 6.1).

Identify training needs and implement a training plan (clause 6.2).

Maintain training records and review the effectiveness of training (clause 6.2).

Identify the infrastructure requirements necessary, and build a business case for implementing these requirements (clause 6.3).

Establish work environment requirements (clause 6.4).

Define product realization process requirements (clause 7.1).

Map the customer management process including contract negotiations, handling inquiries, complaint processing, communications, and records (clause 7.2.3).

Map the design and development process as per clause 7.3.

Identify the necessary records for design and development control (clause 7.4).

Map the purchasing process as per clause 7.4.

Establish criteria for evaluating and selecting suppliers (for example, use an approved supplier list (clause 7.4.2).

Establish process controls for core business process (for example, in a manufacturing company the production process) (clause 7.5.1).

Identify processes where the resulting output cannot be verified by subsequent monitoring or measurement, and implement the necessary controls (clause 7.5.2).

Identify requirements for identification, traceability, and inspection, and test status and implement the necessary controls. Refer to in-house needs, legislation, and customer needs (clause 7.5.3).

If customers supply intellectual property, materials, components, or products, establish the controls required (clause 7.5.4).

Implement the controls necessary to protect raw materials, components, and products from damage and/or deterioration (clause 7.5.5).

Implement the necessary storage controls (clause 7.5.5).

Implement the necessary packaging controls (clause 7.5.5).

Implement the necessary preservation controls (clause 7.5.5).

Develop a process for selecting inspection and test equipment (clause 7.6).

Maintain an equipment register (clause 7.6).

Identify calibration process as per clause 7.6 and the necessary requirements for traceability to national and international standards.

Establish the calibration records required (clause 7.6).

Identify the processes necessary to demonstrate conformity of the product, to ensure conformity of the quality management system, and to continually improve the effectiveness of the quality management system (clause 8.1).

Define processes for measuring customer satisfaction and for responding to findings (clause 8.2.1).

Develop purpose and objectives for the audit process (clause 8.2.2).

Implement a documented procedure for internal audits (clause 8.2.2).

Train auditors (clause 8.2.2).

Define all process measurement and monitoring methods including acceptance criteria, frequency of checks, responsibilities, criticality of checks, and action in the event errors are detected (clause 8.2.3).

Define all product measurement and monitoring methods including acceptance criteria, frequency of checks, responsibilities, criticality of checks, and action in the event errors are detected (clause 8.2.4).

Establish records required for process and product monitoring and measurement (clauses 8.2.3 and 8.2.4).

Implement a documented procedure for the control of nonconforming product as per clause 8.3 (including supplier-related problems, in-house problems, concessions/waivers, product recall, and customer returns).

Ensure that records related to nonconforming product complete the cycle of disposition (clause 8.3).

Identify the internal and external data essential for the successful operation of the business and define processes for capturing and disseminating those data (clause 8.4).

Define processes for continual improvement (clause 8.5.1).

Implement documented procedures for corrective action focused on eliminating the recurrence of problems (clause 8.5.2).

Implement documented procedures for preventive action focused on eliminating potential causes of problems (clause 8.5.3).

Job Description for an Internal Auditor

JOB DESCRIPTION FOR AN INTERNAL AUDITOR

Reporting to the internal audit program manager

Department: Various

Purpose: To ensure that the quality management system is evaluated for effectiveness, conformity, and opportunities for improvement and that corrective action is verified for implementation, effectiveness, and sustainability.

The Role Model

Conducts internal audits as scheduled and prepares clear reports that indicate the extent of conformity with specified requirements, areas of conformity and nonconformity, and opportunities for improvement

Tasks

Participates in the scheduling of internal audits

Conducts initial preparation and research of areas/processes to be audited, including internal and external factors

Prepares checklists covering the scope and objectives of the audit

Liaisons with process owners

Executes internal audits including interviewing and examination of documents, records, and products

Presents findings to management representatives

Prepares audit reports and, where necessary, nonconformity reports

Follows up corrective action to determine implementation and continued effectiveness

Participates in internal auditor network meetings as a means of continually improving the internal audit process

Internal Contacts

Potentially all departmental/process personnel

External Contacts

Customer representatives

Third-party auditors

Knowledge Required

Task	Knowledge
Participate in the scheduling of internal audits	ISO 9001/ISO 19011 Company system
Conduct initial preparation and research of areas/processes to be audited, including internal and external factors	Business objectives Business processes
Prepare checklists covering the scope and objectives of the audit	Questioning techniques
Liaison with process owners	Business process model
Execute internal audits including interviewing and examination of records, products, and documents	Record taking Interview techniques Business record requirements
Present findings to management representatives	Interpersonal skills Presentation skills
Prepare audit reports and, where necessary, nonconformity reports	Report writing
Follow up corrective action to determine implementation and continued effectiveness	The nature of corrective action
Participate in internal auditor network meetings as a means of continually improving the internal audit process	Meetings skills Continual improvement tools

Hazards and Skills to Deal with Them

Hazard	Skill
General health and safety	Health and safety training.
Stress	Managing conflicts

Budgetary Authority

As defined in the annual budget process

Measures of Performance

Value-adding contribution of audit findings—evaluated as part of the appraisal process

Agreed: .... Date: ....

Agreed: .... Date: ....

Bibliography

Deming, W. Edwards. *Out of the Crisis*. Cambridge, Massachusetts: MIT Press, 2000.

Eurospan Developments Ltd. QMS Auditor/Lead Auditor Course 2000 (training course material). IRCA A17084.

International Organization for Standardization. ISO 9000:2000, *Quality management systems—Fundamentals and vocabulary*.

———. ISO 9001:2000, *Quality management systems—Requirements*.

———. ISO 9004:2000, *Quality management systems—Guidelines for performance improvements*.

———. ISO 10011/19011, *Guidelines for quality and/or environmental management systems auditing*.

———. Records required by ISO 9001:2000 Document: ISO/TC176/SC2/N525R, Annex B. www.iso.ch (Accessed August 2001).

International Register of Certificated Auditors IRCA 2245 certification criteria for the ISO 9000:2000 series Auditor/Lead Auditor Training Course.

O'Hanlon, Tim. *Auditor Líder*. São Paulo: Pioneira, 1994.

Russell, J. P., and Terry Regel. *After the Quality Audit: Closing the Loop on the Audit Process*. 2nd ed. Milwaukee, WI: ASQ Press, 2000.

Further Reading

Arter, Dennis R. *Quality Audits for Improved Performance*. 2nd ed. Milwaukee, WI: ASQ Press, 1994.

Russell, J. P., ed. *Quality Audit Handbook*. 2nd ed. Milwaukee, WI: ASQ Press, 2000.

ASQ Quality Audit Technical Committee. *How to Plan an Audit*. Edited by Charles B. Robinson. Milwaukee, WI: ASQ Press, 1987.

Keeney, Kent A. *ISO 9000 Auditor's Companion*. Milwaukee, WI: ASQC Quality Press, 2001.

Sayle, Allan J. *Management Audits: The Assessment of Quality Management Systems*. 3rd ed. Milwaukee, WI: ASQ Press, 1997.

Index

Page numbers in **bold** indicate figure entry